A Fine Romance

Because nothing happens unless
first we dream. ♥ CARL SANDBURG

Nor would I miss the early
darkness & the pleasant
firelight tea and long evenings
among my books.
♥ Elizabeth von Arnim

MY BOOK

A FINE ROMANCE

Go, little book,
& wish to all
Flowers
in the garden,
meat in the hall,
A bin of wine,
A spice of wit,
A house with lawns enclosing it,
A living river by the door,
A nightingale in the sycamore!

Robert Louis Stevenson

Falling in Love with

THE ENGLISH COUNTRYSIDE

A Fine Romance

Susan Branch

SPRING STREET
Publishing

MARTHA'S VINEYARD · MASSACHUSETTS

Spring Street Publishing
P O B O X 2 4 6 3
VINEYARD HAVEN, MA
0 2 5 6 8
sales@springstreetpublishing.com

F I R S T E D I T I O N
ISBN 978-0-9960440-4-2

Library of Congress Control Number
2017901426

10 9 8 7 6 5

RRD-IN

PRINTED IN THE
UNITED STATES OF AMERICA

Dedication

Normally I dedicate my diaries to the darkest corner of my closet where they live on a shelf in perpetual embarrassment (likely kicking up their heels & dancing in the dark, but not so that anyone can see).

> 21 July 1987 11:30am
>
> What a DOLL!
>
> He is a Doll.
> He is too much too perfect
> I have to pinch myself &
> him — to make sure he's real.
> He is a darling Doll.
> He makes me Hip Hop Happy.

But this diary is different, written to memorialize a dream-come-true & dedicated with all my heart to

Joe Hall, the love of my life, without whom there's an unending list of what might not have been. We're like a recipe, he & I; I'm the cream, he's the honey, & this trip through the English countryside was our cup of tea.

i think it bespeaks a generous nature, a man who can cook. ♥ JILLY COOPER

Oh yes, he can cook too. I hope I'm not giving away too much of the love story that starts on page thirteen by including this excerpt from my diary. I still feel exactly the same way I did all those years ago. Did I mention he's a Doll?

I would also like to give a grateful & humble bow to the fickle hand of fate. *Thank you*

Scotland

LAKE DISTRICT
Ambleside
4

Yorkshire 5
Dales

York
6

Winksworth
3

England

Ireland

Wales

Bibury
7

Aylesbury
2

London

Tetbury
8

Chawton
9

Tenterden
1

FRANCE

Queen Mary 2

THERE ARE NO RULES of ARCHITECTURE for A CASTLE IN THE CLOUDS. ♥ G.K. CHESTERTON

Note to Gentle Readers (and all the rest of you, too ♥.): When you see a star ★ in the text it means I have a lot more information for you. Go to www.susanbranch.com for LINKS, listed both by page number and alphabetically. Click on "I LOVE ENGLAND," then on "APPENDIX." ♥

Contents

You can never get a cup of tea large enough or a book long enough to suit me.
♥ C.S. LEWIS

Sing me an old-fashioned song...

The only thing better than singing is more singing. ♥ *Ella Fitzgerald*

The sheet music (© 1936) for *A Fine Romance*, words by Dorothy Fields & music by Jerome Kern, was used by kind permissions of Shapiro, Bernstein & Co., Inc. o/b/o Aldi Music & Davis Wright Tremaine LLP. All rights reserved.

Glory Days by Bruce Springsteen. Copyright © 1984 Bruce Springsteen (ASCAP). Reprinted by permission. International copyright secured. All rights reserved.

(Love is) The Tender Trap, words by Sammy Cahn, music by James Van Heusen. Copyright © 1955 (renewed), Barton Music Corp. All rights reserved. Used by permission. Reprinted with permission of Hal Leonard Corporation.

Poetry Man, words & music by Phoebe Snow. Copyright © 1973 Almo Music Corp. Copyright renewed. All rights reserved. Used by permission. Reprinted with permission of Hal Leonard Corporation.

I wish I could write a beautiful book to break those hearts that are soon to cease to exist: a book of faith & small neat worlds & of people that live by the philosophies of popular songs. ♥ *Zelda Fitzgerald*

Friends, they are kind to each other's hopes. They cherish each other's dreams.

♥ Henry David Thoreau

I'd like to thank my friends & family for being so very kind to my hopes over the years. Sending special hugs to Kellee Rasor, Alfredo Jimenez, Sheri Honeycutt, Judy Watkins, Peg Ackerman, Gary Gatel, & Elaine Sullivan: I couldn't have done this book without you. My mom & dad too, who've been my biggest supporters all my life. To my brothers & sisters (especially my sister Shelly who's forced to put up with me more than the others). To my friends in Martha's Vineyard, California & England for allowing me to be M.I.A. long enough to write this book.

LET'S GO TO LUNCH!

And to my Blog Girlfriends who, in a virtual way, were with us every day of our trip to England, squeezing themselves into suitcases, stowing away on the ship, & sending me notes of encouragement while I finished the book—THIS ONE'S for YOU!

AND NOW FOR A

DISCLAIMER

The words contained in the following pages are true to the best of my knowledge. If I've made a mistake, gentle reader, please remember the famous quote from *Bridget Jones Diary*, "It's just a diary — everyone knows diaries are full of crap."

Thank you!

The Management

BEATRIX POTTER'S DIARY

Secret Garden

WILDFLOWERS

Howards End

PRIDE & PREJUDICE

Tea in the Garden

THE COTSWOLDS

BIRDS

Portrait of a Marriage

If there were dreams to sell,
   merry & sad to tell,
& the crier rang his bell,
   what would you buy?
         Thomas Beddoes

PREFACE

This diary was written in May and June of 2012, but before we begin, let's take a little trip back in time and head to the magical island of Martha's Vineyard, to a beautiful early-fall evening in 1986.

Imagine you are standing outside a two-story, white-painted, New England building, just a block from the sea; leaves are drifting down, you taste salt air, you see the first star, and of course you make a wish: you wish the whole world could be as happy as you are at this moment. You smell garlic cooking & you hear the screen door clap behind you as you walk into a large, airy restaurant with wooden floors & high ceilings. Tall, old-fashioned double-hung windows are wide open along three sides of the room. A comfortably cool harbor breeze brushes over diners chatting at the white-draped tables; the clatter of silverware, sparkle of candlelight on wine glasses; fragrance of basil scenting the air; young servers in long white aprons carry bowls of steaming clams & plates with bright red lobster claws dangling over the edge; there's a large tree in the center of the room; under it is a very hip-looking New York kind of guy, waiting to put your name

11

on the list for a table, but you want a seat at the clam bar, don't you, because that's where the action is . . .

I thought you might like to see the true beginning of the story... how I met Joe & how this Diary came to be.

I hope you like love stories!

Across the gateway of my heart, I wrote 'No thoroughfare' But love came laughing by and cried, 'I enter everywhere.'

♥ Herbert Shipman

12

A FINE ROMANCE

FALLING IN LOVE AGAIN

QUEEN ELIZABETH

*W*ISHING AND WANTING TO SEE YOU, I STEP ON THIN ICE. ♥*Madoka Mayuzumi*

The first present Joe ever gave me started out as a souvenir cufflink from the RMS *Queen Elizabeth*; he had it made into a charm for my bracelet and gave it to me at the beginning of our budding relationship.

It made perfect sense considering what went on between us the night we met, on a beautiful evening at the end of summer, in a restaurant on Martha's Vineyard (where we live) called The Ocean Club. I was sitting on a high wooden stool at the clam bar, talking to the girlfriend I'd come with. We sat across the counter from an aproned bartender who was shucking oysters and placing them on a plate of crushed ice; he stood in front of a huge gilt-edged mirror that reached to the ceiling, reflecting tall open windows that went all the way around the room. Two guys sat down at the bar on the empty stools next to us. I knew one of them; I leaned forward on the bar to see around the tall one wearing the black beret to say hello to the one I knew; and, over restaurant clatter of silverware, conversation, and music, he introduced me to the stranger whose name was Joe.

Joe: IT WAS LOVE AT FIRST SIGHT. I EVEN REMEMBER WHAT SHE WAS WEARING: A LONG NARROW SKIRT WITH A WIDE LEATHER BELT AND A WHITE LINEN SHIRT.

Me: I THINK YOU SHOULD LET ME TELL IT.

Since our shoulders were practically rubbing together, it was inevitable that we should begin talking. We were friendly and chatty, as people are in this kind of situation. Just shooting the breeze.

For a little background, this pleasant encounter took place at about the same time I had decided I was finished with men

FOREVER. My heart had become tattered by life; a sad divorce, five years earlier, had left me devastated and feeling like a nobody. Then, after years of trying to find love again with no luck at all, I'd finally given up. It was all too fraught with danger. No more, I said to the wallpaper in my kitchen, toasting myself with my tea cup in the reflection of my kitchen window. It definitely wasn't the way I thought my life would go – or how I WANTED it to go – but obviously I was meant to be alone. Childless and deep into my thirties, I'd come to terms with it. I'd had to find other things to want and care about when I rebuilt my life.

I DIDN'T REALLY LIVE ALONE.

Besides, I had more than my share of blessings; I had a tiny, one-bedroom house in the woods, "out of the wind's and the rain's way," that I could decorate any way I wanted. It had a garden where wild blueberries grew, and a walk I could go on every day, out a dirt road to the water. I had three kitties. I was fine. Plus, at the time I met Joe, I was eagerly anticipating the publication of my first cookbook, coming out at the end of October. These were enough miracles for me. A person shouldn't be greedy.

"It is overdoing the thing to die of love."
♥ French Proverb

♪ **WHAT'S LOVE GOT TO DO, GOT TO DO WITH IT...** ♪

Knew all the words to this song that was playing in the restaurant that night. 💙

Joe seemed nice; he was friendly; it wasn't long before he was feeding me from his plate (because that's just what he does!). He was five years younger than me, a baby. A very cute, tall baby, but still, a baby.

Even though I'd been told by two different psychics that I was going to fall in love with a tall man with a beard, and even though Joe was tall and had a beard, I did not recognize him. I discounted what they said because I really wasn't a beard person. And even though, years before, I had written in my diary that the perfect man for me would be "a 6'2" Leo who can cook", and even though Joe told me he had a Leo birthday, and that he ran the Black Dog, a famous local restaurant, where he was also the chef, still, I did not recognize him.

Our conversation that night went everywhere. I learned that he loved Fred Astaire & Ginger Rogers. (Have I told you I love Fred Astaire & Ginger Rogers? I do! I love old movies!) No man I'd ever had a relationship with even knew who Fred & Ginger were! Joe had Fred Astaire albums! When he told me he'd sailed on a ship to England with his mother when he was twelve, I was so impressed — I'd always wanted to do that. Lots of my favorite old movies had glamorous ocean-liner adventure in them, movies like *An Affair to Remember*, *The Lady Eve*, & *Shall We Dance*; I'd dreamed of it since I was young. We talked about that a lot, how much each of us would like to go to Europe on a ship (separately, of course).

The conversation was fun; we talked about the pesto we were eating, a new thing on the island at the time; but he was still too young for me; besides, and most importantly, I had convinced myself there was never going to be

17

any more love in my life. I liked the feeling that decision had given me; my heart was now safe, protected from the ravages of unreliable love.

After that night, we ran into each other a couple of times; it's a small island. We said hello, but not much more; always nice, but nothing to write home about, to which my best friend Diana could attest because I never wrote home about him.

Joe: I WAS TOTALLY SMITTEN WITH HER BUT I WAS IN THE MIDST OF ENDING A RELATIONSHIP & COULDN'T ASK HER OUT. Me: WHATEVER.
(DID HE SAY "SMITTEN"?)

Several months went by. The leaves came down, my first book was published; winter set in, the snow began to fall, and one stormy day at the end of January, feeling house-bound, I took myself down to the Black Dog for lunch, something I did all the time. I loved to bring along a stack of magazines and settle in for a bowl of chowder at a table in front of the fire and while away a snowy afternoon, people-watching, alone, just me, myself, and I, and whatever home decorating magazine I had at the moment.

Suddenly, out from somewhere behind the kitchen, came Joe. I'd never seen him there before. "Hello, hello," we say, but then he asks, "Mind if I sit down?"

The chair scrapes against the wood floor, and he is sitting, still wearing that cute black beret. Glancing longingly at my magazine, feeling a little bit interrupted from my happy anonymous reverie, I turn my face to his to hear what the heck he wants.

He then proceeds to tell me he has tickets to the Boston Symphony the first week-end in February, and asks me to go with him! To Boston! For the weekend!

He said it so casually, as if it was perfectly normal! I didn't know WHAT to say because I had no excuse ready; but of course, I'm not going to Boston *for the weekend* with a perfect stranger I've barely met who could be an ax-murderer for all I know.

The problem was (and is), a lie shows in my eyes like cherries coming up in a slot machine. I don't make eye contact; I stammer, blink too much & go blank ~ I can *feel* the word LIAR ticker-tape across my forehead. I avoid lying unless I'm fully prepared to accept an Academy Award for my performance, which could never happen unless I had time to rehearse. I don't like hurting people's feelings right to their faces! Long before this moment, I had made a rule: ALWAYS SAY 'YES' NO MATTER WHAT. That way, I could go home, "check the calendar," find out I'm "busy," call the person back, & cancel gracefully, saving everyone a lot of embarrassment.

So that was the plan. "Yes, I'd love it," I said, enthusiastically, "sounds like fun," la-la-la, we agreed. He said he'd call, so on and so forth; then he disappeared back into the kitchen, and I happily went back to reading how to make curtains out of an old tablecloth. Not going to Boston.

MY FIRST HOUSE ON MARTHA'S VINEYARD

On the phone, Diana, my best friend in California (where I grew up, and where the terrible sad divorce took place; California, where I ran away from, coming to Martha's Vineyard alone and heart-broken six years before), said, "Is this a date?" "No, it's not a date," I said, "he's too young for me; he probably has nothing else to do, it's winter."

"Then why don't you want to go?" she asked. I explained my stranger/ax-murderer theory; she laughed, "If he was an ax-murderer it would have been in the paper! Besides, there you are, in that little house in the middle of nowhere, surrounded in freezing snow, alone all the time ~ I'm worried about you!

21

And now, you've got this bright-lights, big-city opportunity with a local guy who knows his way around Boston. You're crazy not to go! You don't have to marry him! Get two rooms!"

She was making sense. I always got lost when I went to Boston. Slowly I began to think, maybe I should go. I didn't know why he'd asked ME, but I was pretty sure it wasn't romantic, considering the age difference. And it wasn't like we'd have nothing to talk about. From that first night I knew we had things in common; we were both from big families; Joe's the youngest of five, and I'm the oldest of eight; family antics are always good to talk about in a pinch! And we could talk about food! Of course, we would get two rooms. I LOVED room service! It was winter; I was bored; I would go!

He called a couple days later, kind of late, from a party; I could hear music and people in the background. I let his invitation stand. . .

I didn't try to get out of it. I felt like a presuming idiot asking for two rooms because in my heart I knew this was just a friendship thing for him, too. And, of course, he was fine with it, "no problem." The perfect gentleman. Later I found out he'd had "a couple of beers" at this party.

Joe: I DO NOT REMEMBER THAT PHONE CALL. SHE IS MAKING THIS PART UP.

It's freezing on February 6 when he picks me up to go to the ferry. We're covered from head to toe in sweaters, scarves, hats, gloves, and overcoats. He's wearing the black beret he always wears (it has that little piece that sticks up on top called a *cabillou* in the *Bernaise* language of southwest France where berets are made, which translates to "small tail" and adds to the *joie de vivre* of this little hat—

23

a hat that would look silly on anyone I knew in California, but on him, it looked adorable. Scientifically speaking, I should say, as a detached observer & appreciator of fashion).

Across the water we went, bobbing in the dark, storm-churned sea, salt spray washing over the windows, blurring lighthouses and coastlines.

We ran into an old friend of Joe's & sat down with her in the warm snack bar, at one of the booths that lined the walls of the large square room on the top of the boat. It was a big help, having her there, she buffered us from too much awkwardness & made conversation easy. I only managed to embarrass myself once while on the boat. I was wearing a heavy denim skirt, snug around the hips, dropping to a long gathered skirt, which buttoned on the side. With it, I wore a soft leather belt which had a funny horn clasp that worked like this:

↙ LAURA ASHLEY SLIP!

As I'm drawing this belt, which I still have, I am thinking. Why did I ever buy this crazy thing?
Oh! I know!
BECAUSE iT'S CUTE!

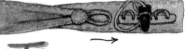

That large loop fits over one of the small loops; the tethered horn slips in to anchor it.

(Or not . . .)

I had gotten up to put cream in my coffee, was standing at the kiosk in the middle of the room, and my cute belt just FELL OFF. It dropped like a rock to the floor with a clunk. It took a moment for it to register. I looked down & there it was at my feet; it felt like my underwear had fallen down! I bent over and pulled it up. I don't think anyone noticed, but that didn't stop my cheeks from turning bright red.

Forty-five minutes later, we pulled into a slip in Woods Hole on Cape Cod. Once docked, we said goodbye to Joe's friend, climbed into the car Joe kept parked there, & drove the two-hour trip, past frosted leafless trees, black against a sky the color of cigarette smoke, up Route 28 to Boston.
We're on our own.

Conversation turns out to be easy; there are no uncomfortable silences. We find we have a lot of little things in common. Besides Fred Astaire (which, you have to admit, is not your normal guy thing) & ocean-liner dreams, we discover our mothers have the same maiden names! On top of that, his post office box is 6324 and mine's 2463!
The plot was thickening...
If he's got an ax on him, I haven't seen it.

OUR ROOM

SCENE OF CRIME

We arrive in Boston. Joe checks in at the hotel reception desk while I wander around the lobby looking at the wallpaper, warming myself in front of the fire. The bellman takes us to the top floor & shows us to a large corner room with its own fireplace.

Joe tips the bellman who turns to leave, & Joe follows him right out the door, saying he's going to park the car! This all happens fast, before I can say, "Where's my room?" Which I didn't want to say in front of the bellman anyway. I'm alone in the room! Immediately, I call Diana in California!

She picks up, "Hello?"
I launch right in; time is of the essence.
"He only got one room!"
I'm standing at a tall picture window, looking out at the view of the city, lights twinkling in the windows of the skyscrapers, watching snow flakes twirling and drifting down.
"What'll I do?"

26

$\mathcal{S}$he instantly gets the gravity of the situation.

"Where is he?"

"He went to park the car."

"How's it going so far?"

"It's good, it's fine, no problem. But only one room."

"How big is it?"

"Big."

"One bed or two?"

"One."

"King size?"

"Uh-huh."

"Which jammies did you bring?"

"The big flannel ones; it's like 30 degrees here."

"Are there robes in the room?"

"Wait a minute, I'm looking...yeah, white terry cloth."

"Perfect, those are like armor."

"So, what'll I do?"

"Nothing. You're fine. This isn't a date, he's just a friend, right?"

"Right...but..."

"You can sleep in the same bed with a friend, it's no big thing. Like a little brother."

"Yeeeaaahhh? Really?...OK, I guess you're right, I can do that."

$\mathcal{O}$f course! What was I thinking?
Diana is right! I'm making a

mountain out of a molehill. Maybe he forgot about the room; maybe it had to do with money or something. He's young; I should be a good sport; I don't want to embarrass him. I have four brothers; I can do this; he's not even interested in me that way.

I found plenty of plausible excuses, settled myself down and was fairly calm by the time I heard my friend and little brother put the key in the door.

In walked Joe, pink-cheeked from the cold, his long black overcoat and cute beret were sprinkled with snowflakes. His arms were filled with flowers, dozens of tulips & bright daffodils in all colors, sparkling with melting snow, filling the room with the fragrance of spring. From the deep pocket of his overcoat, he pulled out a bottle of champagne.

Oh oh, I thought . . .

this looks like trouble . . .

That weekend we walked all over Boston in our big coats, scarves blowing out behind us, glove-in-glove. On the way back to the hotel★ that first night after dinner, in a light snowfall, under twinkle-lighted trees in Boston Common, he kissed me & it wasn't like a brother, & not all that child-like either. But we continued to keep a respectful distance as people normally would when they're surprised to find themselves on a first date in 1987.

On Saturday night, instead of going to the concert (neither of us wanted to anymore), Joe took us to dinner at a small candle-lit bistro on Berkeley Street. He wore a coat & tie; waiters in long white aprons draped linen napkins across our laps. We both ordered the same thing, which I will never forget because we did the same thing we've done at every dinner since, analyzed the food, figuring out what was in it so we could make it later, at home. If you've ever made the Steak au Poivre* in my book *Vineyard Seasons*, you know how delicious our dinner was that night.

Later, we stepped out of the cozy restaurant into the clean, cold air under a starry sky to walk back to the hotel. We heard something like bells or music & began to move toward it. As we rounded the corner, we were delighted to see the entire Boston Police Department bagpipe band, the Gaelic Column of Pipes & Drums, marching down the middle of deserted Newbury Street, practicing for the St. Patrick's Day Parade!

The high, tinny, strange & somehow touching music filled the air, echoing through the dark, empty city streets. The drummers twirled their sticks as they marched; they played Danny Boy...

♫ 'Tis I'll be here in sunshine or in shadow...

Something else we have in common, we both like bagpipes. It felt like a blessing. And then it was time to go home & back to real life. The day after that, my mom arrived on the island to stay with me for a ten-day visit.

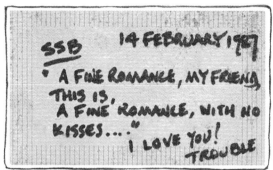

SSB   14 FEBRUARY 1987

" A FINE ROMANCE, MY FRIEND,
THIS IS,
A FINE ROMANCE, WITH NO
KISSES...."
        I LOVE YOU!
                TROUBLE

THIS CARD WOULD LOOK A LOT BETTER IF IT
HADN'T SPENT 10 YEARS ON THE FRIDGE.♥

J oe called a couple of times during the ten days; he stopped over once or twice to say hello while my mom was there. He took us out to dinner. On Valentine's Day, he brought me a Fred Astaire album. The card (it came with roses!) was sweet but it had the word "love" on it! SCARY! I was struggling to stay sensible; I was so happy my mom was there to be my chaperone. Despite the Valentines & the dinner, Joe seemed to be busy & even a little bit distant during those ten days, which I found somewhat confusing, but it didn't matter; I was trying NOT to think about him as I was still, at heart, through with love.

: I WANTED TO GIVE YOU TIME TO BE WITH YOUR MOM.

(Let's not forget the final touches on the breakup with the other girl...as I found out later!)

Joe: OH YEAH.

MOM: WASN'T THAT *THOUGHTFUL*?

(She only heard the part about the "time with your mom.")

My mother loved Joe at first sight. She thought he was perfect, except, that week, he didn't call often enough.

"I wonder why he doesn't call?" she said. (A lot.)

I should never have told her, I thought.

She's in the green chair, knitting. I'm sitting at the table with my watercolors, painting. It's snowing outside, there's a fire in the fireplace, *Sabrina,* with Audrey Hepburn, is on TV. My mom wanted to talk about Joe, & so she did.

"Wasn't that *thoughtful* of him to take us *both* to dinner? He seems so nice, such a *gentleman.* I think he's crazy about you!

"Did you say he's the youngest of five? Like our Brad. You two have *so much* in common!" (Quiet.) "Have you met his parents?"

"Not yet, Mom." *His parents!* She's killing me. The knitting needles are clicking... she goes on...

"I know he likes you; he was so attentive at dinner." She looks at me over her glasses.

"I don't understand why he hasn't called. He must be really busy! I can't believe he manages that restaurant *all by himself!*" (My mom doesn't get out much.)

Wrapping the yarn around the knitting needle, she looks up perkily and asks, "What time is it?" I start to look at the clock; she goes on, "Maybe he'll call after lunch." She cocks her head, "Oh! Did you hear that? Is that a car?"

"Mom, please." I say. "You have to quit bringing him up. I don't even know if I like him. I don't want to sit around here all the time, wondering what he's doing. Please quit talking about him."

"Oh. OK. I'm sorry." (Very busy with the knitting.) Now I feel bad.
"You don't have to be sorry."

We are quiet while she knits & I paint. Sabrina is waiting for her dad at the train station, just back from Paris, looking so chic with her haircut & her poodle. I'm not thinking about Joe, I'm listening to the movie. The fire is popping softly, knitting needles are clicking, Sabrina's in the car with David now, teasing him, not telling him who she is. I'm painting a basket of apples that's sitting on the table; a drop of red paint spreads on the wet watercolor paper. "Maybe he's..." my mom starts, then, realizing what she's doing, she claps her mouth shut & guilt floods her face.

33

Too late; I look up at her without moving my head; I can't help but laugh; I'm thinking about him again.

After a wonderful visit, my darling little mommy goes back home to California. Joe calls that morning and of course I invite him to dinner.

He knocks on the door & the cold air that comes in with his tall self makes the candle flames waver. He dwarfs my tiny house with the low ceilings into a doll house. He gives me a bouquet of yellow daffodils. I hang his beret on the back of the door.

"It smells great in here," he says.

We eat in front of the fire. We talk, we laugh, we play old music; Frank Sinatra sings ♪ YOU SEE A PAIR OF LAUGHING EYES ♫ AND SUDDENLY YOU'RE SIGHING SIGHS... ♪

Joe & Mom

Joe puts another log on the fire; we eat Apple Crisp, we pour more wine. And that night, Joe becomes The Man Who Came to Dinner... and Never Left.

A few days later, I phoned my mom to tell her "he called!"

She was so happy!

34

SNOOKUMS
IZZY WIZZY WOO?
KUTCHIE KOOTCHIE

xxx J.

WE SEEM TO SPEAK THE SAME LANGUAGE

TALK TO ME SOME MORE,
YOU DON'T HAVE TO GO
YOU'RE THE POETRY MAN.
Phoebe Snow
It took a while, but Joe made me believe in love again. Sometimes when we're mad at each other, if we just remember to tell the story of our first date, by the time he comes into the hotel room, arms overflowing with flowers, we're good again.

Sweeeeeeetness!

Years after we met, Joe recited his childhood bedtime prayer in a rote, memorized, sing-song way. (He had me at "Puddikins.")

"God bless Mommy & Daddy, Steve & Betsey, Nancy & Tom, John & Michael & Joey (himself), Susi (poodle), Nosey, Inky, Puddikins, Sammy, Georgia, Triscuit; all my friends & all my relations. And make me a good boy. Amen."

US, IN BATH, ENGLAND; 2004 (say it "Bawth")

SAIL AWAY WITH ME

In 2004, Joe & I realized the ocean-liner dream of our first meeting & sailed to England on the *Queen Elizabeth 2* for the most wonderful adventure of our lives: two months wandering the beautiful back roads of rural England! It was perfection, a dream-come-true; eye opening & a life changer for us. ♥

Since 2004, we've yearned to go back & do it again, but we always seem to come up with reasons why 'NOW' is never the right time.

36

Fast forward to freezing February 2012. We're in front of the fire in our old house on Martha's Vineyard, celebrating the 25th anniversary of our first date that never ended. ♥

Joe looked up from his steak au poivre & scalloped potatoes & said, ♥

"Why don't we go back to England? I mean really; let's really go!" ♥

"What are you thinking?" I say, sitting up straight. "When?"

"Now. Soon—." ♥

"You mean, like spring? That's like tomorrow!" (I say 'like' a lot.) ♥

"Yes! Let's do it!" He's darn sure of himself all of a sudden.
"We keep talking about it, but we don't do anything. We've put it off long enough — let's go now — while we're healthy, our families are healthy — don't worry, the cats will be fine! We should go now!" ♥

"For how long?" I'm trying to visualize this; Joe's somewhat retired but I'm in the middle of projects.

BREAKING AWAY FROM NORMAL

37

WHO WILL THROW MY BALL?

Jack

"Let's go in May," he said, "come home the end of June; two months, like last time."

"Oh honey," I'm shaking my head, "I don't really think we can do that."

CUE THE MUSIC

Glory days, well they'll pass you by ♪
Glory days, in the wink of a young girl's eye...
♪ BRUCE SPRINGSTEEN

But the idea wouldn't go away. We dreamed out loud. We talked about it on our morning walks, weighing the pros & cons. It was obvious we should not go. First off, we shouldn't spend the money; plus, I have a book to finish; Jack, our kitten, is only seven months old; go for two months? Who will plant the garden; who will take off the storm windows?

Every discussion of the reasons we absolutely could not go ended up with, "But wouldn't it be FUN?"

Early April, I turned 65!

GLORY DAYS
PASSING BY

I thought, for the thousandth time, how much I've always dreamed of going up to the Lake District to see Beatrix Potter's house... a watercolor artist whose life I admire.

Girl Kitty

HAVE I MENTIONED LATELY HOW MUCH
I LOVE SLEEPING WITH YOU?

38

Joe says, "This time we should explore the Lake District & go to Beatrix Potter's House."

Well, that did it. Joe called Cunard ✱ & made reservations for a stateroom on the Queen Mary 2. We started making lists, arranging places to stay, finding a house/kitty-sitter (& ball thrower); shopping & packing, with butterfly stomachs, in a bit of a tizzy. Ocean liner. OMG.

Time is such a funny thing; one minute it's forever & the next, it's gone.

Bold, mature, well-thought-out, last-minute decision made, we're set to depart from New York on May 4, 2012. For the next eight weeks, I'll be keeping this diary as the trip unfolds; we want you to come along — just say Yes!

This book begins in the past; it's going to end up in the future; and what happens next is still a mystery. Fun, huh?

As I'm writing this, it's May 2; we're leaving to drive to New York tomorrow! You should go pack — find your passport!

HERE WE GO....
YIKES!
and
¡OH BOY!

Twenty years from now, you will be more disappointed by the things you didn't do than by the ones you did.

Sail away from the safe harbor.

Catch the trade winds in your sails.

EXPLORE.

Dream.

Discover.

Mark Twain

BON VOYAGE

MAY 3. Said goodbye to everyone; left the island this afternoon, driving to New York. We're in Connecticut now, stopped for the night; having dinner in front of the fire at the Griswold Inn. Joe has a Pimm's Cup* to go with his *New York Times*; my new diary and I are sipping on a glass of cold rosé. The ship leaves tomorrow night but we board around 1 pm. SO EXCITED.

The hardest thing was kissing the kitties goodbye. When I came into the kitchen this morning, Jack was hanging by his front paws from the open silverware drawer. He looked so cute with his little Hercule Poirot mustache, I almost had to cancel the trip! I could barely get Girl out of my suitcase ~ I left our worn T-shirts & jammies on all their favorite napping places ~ so they can sleep on them & have our scent & know we're coming back. I have to quit thinking about them. They're in good hands ~ our house-sitter, Will, has stayed with them before; he'll take good care of them.

She (the cat) hasn't had her full ration of kisses-on-the-lips today. ...she had the half-past-six one in the garden, but she's missed tonight's.
♥ Colette

41

May 3, cont.

When I went on my first date with Joe, I asked him, "What shall I bring?" He answered, "Everything."

And that has been the modus operandi for our traveling life ever since: just bring it all! This time we may have gone too far. There almost wasn't room for me in the car! We packed two computers, two phones, two cameras with batteries, a travel printer, a power strip, extension cords, & battery-chargers for everything. We have music CDs, videos, an electric tea kettle, our mugs, a canister of my favorite lavender-Earl Grey tea (that I really can't live without) & Joe's favorite, PG Tips (because everyone knows how hard it is to find tea in England!). Oh well! We're ready for anything!

We also brought our own American-style measuring cups & spoons. We'll be staying in apartments & cottages; we'll have kitchens; we can cook - we won't have to eat out all the time; it'll be more homey.

I brought my pillow, of course, not going anywhere without my pillow; brought my watercolors so I can paint these little drawings whenever we get settled; I have my knitting, my green plaid shawl & we brought "Petey," the doll Joe got on his first crossing with his mom when he was a kid; we have a bag of travel books, evening clothes for the ship ~ the basic necessities of life for a two-month trip abroad...good thing they have no weight limit for luggage aboard the ship!

There's a live band in the bar here; they're playing "There will never be another you."

42

↑
Look! It's the Statue of Liberty!

May 4, Friday, 7PM Sailing Day!

EASTBOUND TRANSATLANTIC CROSSING HAS COMMENCED!

WE'RE ON THE SHIP and it is MOVING!

Right this minute, I'm sitting in a comfy armchair at a cocktail table in front of a tall window in the "Chart Room" ~ other passengers are milling about, wandering in and out, settling on chairs & sofas. I have my diary & my Statue of Liberty pen — I want to write before I forget this amazing day! The OCEAN is right outside my window!

There are people who board this ship & immediately stretch out in a lounge chair on the Promenade Deck & take a nap! That's how calm they are! I don't know how they do it~ they must be seasoned travelers. Not us! We've been running around all day, finding out where everything is ~the Queen's Room, the Spa (Canyon Ranch Spa!), the library, Planetarium!!, dining room; the five pools, the theater ~ the whole thing is wide stairways, swirly patterned carpeting, glass & polished brass. In the gold, mirrored elevator, Frank Sinatra sang, "She gets too hungry for dinner at eight..." ♪

JUST LIKE IN THE MOVIES!

Our stateroom has its own outdoor balcony. There was a bottle of champagne waiting in our room, in an ice bucket, with two glasses!

And look at this corridor~ our stateroom is at the far end. When we turned into this hallway Joe said, "Oops, we must have come up the wrong elevator." Then he looked at me & said, "Would you run down there, stand in front of our room, so I can take your picture?"

"Do you really think it matters if it's me or not?"

44

I ask him. "Can't we just wait for someone to walk by and take their picture and tell everyone it's me?"

"It'd be better if it was you," he said pitifully. So I went. Can you see me? ...No.

I think I might be able to lose some weight on this ship!

WE ARE ROCKING A LITTLE BIT...

We got on board at 1 p.m. & now it's after 8 & we're already late for dinner! It's OK, Joe's still outside with his camera & I'm too excited to eat. Not too excited to drink though – a cocktail waitress from Latvia just brought me a glass of wine. The crew seems to be from everywhere – the passengers, too. Little microcosm of the world.

Here's how it was a couple of hours ago when the _Queen Mary 2_ blasted its horn, long & low, blew a puff of black smoke into the sky & began to move, very slowly down the harbor with the whole city of New York in front of us!!!

B R E A T H T A K I N G

We stood together high up on the Observation Deck & took in the sights — floor after floor of passengers leaning out over balconies, waving, chatting, & taking pictures. Four decks below on the Promenade Deck, joggers ran, couples strolled, children played, groups gathered for photographs & waiters served champagne

from rolling carts to people propped in lounge chairs; with the Empire State Building in the distance, sea-gulls crying & flags flying; horns blowing from tug boats & ferries in salute to the Queen; the luminescent sea & sky, & foamy white trails in the wake of every boat.

AND THEN! AS IF THIS WASN'T ENOUGH...

Just as we were steaming past the Statue of Liberty, the sun came out for the first time today, shining on her starry crown, lighting up New York, & putting a twinkle on the hundreds of champagne glasses dangling over the rails! I looked up at Joe — he was blurry but I could see his eyes were shining with tears, just like mine. He put his arm around me, we clicked glasses ~ PING! He said, "HAPPY ANNIVERSARY, honey" and we agreed that at that moment we felt like the luckiest people in the world.

We picked up speed in the gathering dusk; lights were coming on & the wind began to blow as we made our way down the harbor. I started to get chilly, so I came to the Chart Room & plunked down next to a window to watch our progress. I can already tell this room is going to be my favorite spot. Did I mention there are violins playing in here? Yes, there are! Uniformed waiters are carrying trays of drinks to people on sofas & chairs. The music is playing, ice is tinkling ~ all this in extreme contrast to what's been going on just outside my window.

Ever since we left the dock we've had both the Coast Guard & the NY City Police Department, on boats, in helicopters, escorting us through the harbor. As we went under the Verrazano Narrows Bridge, there was an escort boat with a manned machine gun speeding along next to us, crashing through white caps caused by the wake of our ship. → See?

On this side of the thick pane of salt-sprayed glass there's golden lamplight glinting off mirrors & liquor bottles while violins serenade & cocktails are being served; & out there, it's cold & colorless & there's a machine gun! A little bizarre! A few moments ago, we hit open sea; the escort boat suddenly pulled up & turned back. We're on our own now!

I have to stop for a moment — a woman just walked by wearing a complete sailor outfit — including the hat! And red high heels. I'm drawing her here. I have to show you.

This ship was magnificent in the harbor; even next to New York, she held her own — if you turned her on end, she's as tall as the Empire State Building! But it occurs to me now, as I look out at the pitching waves, we might not be as big as we think we are.

Joe popped in a couple of minutes ago... "Did you see that?" Talking about going under the bridge... "Oh yeah, I saw it!" Off to dinner we go! Byeeee

Cute!

Queen Mary 2
HAMILTON

DAY ONE

May 5, Saturday 5am Dark ♦ Good Morning!

Right now, I'm sunk into the sofa in our cabin with a pillow on my lap, diary on the pillow, writing you. Slept so well; the ship rocks gently and makes creaking noises like an old house settling. Joe's still asleep. I put a pillow around his head to block the light, turned on the lamp in the corner of the room, & boiled water for tea in the kettle we brought along—there's 24 hr. room service here, but it's just easier to do it myself.

FOUND THE BATTERIES!

I opened the door & stepped out onto our deck into cold gusty winds & loud whooshing waves, like being on the inside of a washing machine~I got right back inside! We are not in Kansas anymore! But it's like a cocoon in the room, muffled & quiet. The bed is snug with a puffy duvet, feather pillows, & smooth white sheets.

We managed to get our things tucked away— you would never know there are twelve bags in here! Joe hid every- thing under the bed & behind the drapes; there are lots of drawers & plenty of closet space, too...

49

May 5, cont.... At dinner last night, I realized I won't be losing weight here after all—I'll be lucky if I break even! The dining room is like a glamorous old-style New York nightclub — open, with tables on several levels on two floors, & grand staircases that meet under an enormous stained-glass skylight; white tablecloths, fresh flowers, soft light, waiters, a wine steward, perfect service & a wonderful menu from which we ordered with reckless abandon, blaming it all on the sea air ~ it makes you soooo hungry!

After a delicious dinner topped off with fresh strawberry cream puffs & caffè lattes, we took ourselves for a walk out on deck. The breeze was misty & fresh; the moon was almost full, shimmering on the water, making the white paint on the ship gleam! We felt like movie stars! I would have liked to see us from far away; we must have been beautiful, all lit up, leaving a wide trail of moonlit sea foam behind us.

The sound of the wind and a view of the rolling waves were hypnotic; it gave me chills — everything is so BIG & open & seemingly FOREVER out there.

Arm in arm on this flying ship, we ambled around the Promenade Deck, passing tall windows where, inside, we could see passengers laughing & talking; past the big silver moon we walked, in the salty wind.

SECOND STAR FROM THE RIGHT & STRAIGHT ON 'TIL MORNING.
J.M.Barrie

I hummed the theme from *An Affair to Remember* so no one but Joe could hear. Wouldn't it be great if you could push a button anytime you want & relive your favorite moments in life? Someone should invent this.

Cunard R.M.S. Queen Mary

From Joe's postcard collection

51

May 5, cont. We really liked the English couple (John & Linda from Sussex) who were seated with us at our table last night. Over our Vichyssoises & Tomato Salads Caprese, we talked, among other things, about the difference between a "cruise" & a "crossing."

"A 'cruise' is a form of entertainment," said John, "like Las Vegas. And when it's over, you're back where you started. A 'crossing' is a mode of travel."

An entertaining mode of travel, I'd say. Six days of nothing to do but BE. Read, knit, write in my diary, breathe ocean air, & sleep! And at the end, ENGLAND!

Here's the cocoon; see what I mean? See Petey? Joe's doll? And on the door to the deck is the garland my Twitter friend Janie★ sent us. It says BON VOYAGE. So it's almost like home in here.

Later, 9pm

Today was this: Forty-five minutes on bike in spa; wet, heavy fog on deck; foghorn blowing all day; mesmerizing swells in ocean; lunch in King's Court; nap; tried to work on computer but no bandwidth; started reading a new book written by the same woman who wrote *Enchanted April*, which I LOVED.

Dinner was lobster tails on creamy cabbage salad (like coleslaw) with lime & basil, & chocolate sundaes (to balance out exercise).

Now, in Chart Room in favorite chairs next to window, (*I get no kick* elegant people *from champagne...*) in dinner clothes like Academy Awards, sequins & black tie, chatting, drinking, laughing; so sparkly in here; Joe so handsome; me so lucky.

Here's Aries horoscope this month, my mom sent me before we left:

"ACCORDING TO THE PLANETS, YOU HAVE GROWN A BIT TOO COMFORTABLE WITH THINGS THE WAY THEY ARE. YOUR LIFE NEEDS SHAKING UP."

More Music... ♪ ♩ *It's only a paper moon*...♪

LA LA LA LA LA GOODNIGHT!

53

Sunday, May 6, 7am. In cocoon. Outside, rolling swells with white caps & gray sky. Still chugging along. Joe ordered room service breakfast last night; he ordered Bangers & Beans! Big serving of baked beans on his plate w/ two large sausages and scrambled eggs. Yuk. He got me a toasted English Muffin with jam which I just had with my tea, & now, I'm going back to bed with my book. But first, I think I'll draw a picture of our cabin - (only it's a lot messier than this!)

WA WA

FRIDGE →

TV

ME

JOE

SHOWER

WARDROBE

INFINITY HALLWAY →
ROOM 11025

Later: In Chart Room; finally got ourselves dressed & out.
Did 45 min. bike ride—too windy to walk on deck. Right now sea spray is blowing off gray choppy waves, blurring the window.

They just sounded the noon whistle - I don't know why they call it a "whistle" - it sounds like a noise we'd hear from an inexperienced tuba player! Then the Captain came on the intercom to tell us how things are going, in English, German, & French (our longitude & latitude; how many miles we've gone, how deep the ocean is after we cross the Continental Shelf; & he mentioned that at 4am we passed the site of the *Titanic* sinking...which he didn't really need to bring up). So, it's 55° on deck; moderate gale; barometer holding; wind picking up, but "no worries, she was built for this kind of sea." That's nice to hear.

54

Hard to believe there are so many people on this ship. It's full, which means there are 2,618 passengers and 1,240 officers & crew on board. (We asked.) But it never feels crowded; there are no lines; rarely anyone in the hall but us; we're alone in the elevators—there are empty chairs in this comfortable room right now— I don't know where everybody is – but they have something like fifteen bars and restaurants here, so that could be it–they're all spread out. So civilized!

It would be a lot more civilized if there were "boat kitties" in here. Like they have at the Algonquin Hotel in New York. And maybe "kitty take-out" for naps & sleeping in the cabins. Probably wouldn't please everyone, but it would make me very happy!

Joe likes the idea, too – he's reading his book Britannia in Brief. Every so often, he stops to give me an interesting tidbit about King George V or the Plantagenets. I wonder how long it will be before they start inserting Wikipedia chips into all newborns & do away with books & school completely???

I'm getting boring — going to knit... then lunch... byeee...

THE CHART ROOM

Wouldn't this look better with Kitties? And maybe one, big, sweet-eyed yellow Lab? Yesssss!

Cnt. May 6

Later: **S**itting in the King's Court with Joe, eating tacos (with spicy pulled-pork filling & sour cream!); looking over the Promenade Deck, watching ~~crazy~~ intrepid people outside, walking round & round the ship, being blown almost off their feet by the wind. Sky is getting darker; boat is rocking; sometimes it makes a hard little thud when it hits the water. I need to go get my Sea-Bands. I don't *feel* seasick but I'm not taking any chances.

Walkathon
1.9 laps = 1 km.

Walkathon
3 laps = 1.1 mile

A sign on the Promenade Deck

There are two ladies at a table behind us — they must have heard the Captain's announcement from the bridge because they're talking about the *Titanic* and the 100th anniversary of the sinking, which was just last month... they're wondering how many lifeboats are on board; talking about drowning & survivors. If they were a TV show, I'd change the channel. It never occurred to me to ask how many life boats they have here. Now they're talking about *The Unsinkable Molly Brown* — much better! Loved that movie.

I'm fine — this ship doesn't scare me ~~at all~~ much — I just wish the ocean would get flatter — right now it's at a full boil! OK — here we go, off to count the lifeboats!

May 7 · Monday · 7am
ARE WE THERE YET?

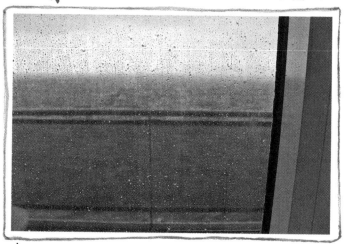

AND WHAT DID WE SEE? WE SAW THE SEA.

Just slept twelve hours! Didn't do too well the rest of yesterday. I was seasick. I put on my wrist bands way too late; next time they go on before I get on the ship, even if the water looks like glass. They usually work for me. Joe's fine; he has permanent sea legs from years of cooking on a schooner, but if the sea is rough, I can even feel queasy during the forty-five-minute ferry ride from Martha's Vineyard to the Mainland.

Feeling better this morning; knitting & having a cup of chamomile tea to soothe my tummy. Joe's sleeping; he went to the casino after tucking me in last night. There's a webcam on the bridge, giving us a constant view of where we're going (unless it's dark); it's a 24-hour TV channel in our room that also plays classical music; it's on now. I see a strip of blue way out there, just above the bobbing horizon, under a sky full of dark clouds.

May 7, continued

should be able to handle this! The sea is in my blood! At least one particle of my DNA came over to America in the form of William Bradford on the *Mayflower*! Those pilgrims did this trip with No luxuries: no wrist bands; no down comforters; no soft, quiet carpeting for bare feet; no room service; probably no violins; no Chart Room (except the real chart room); no bathroom; the trip took over two months, & when they finally landed in Cape Cod Bay, there was no welcome wagon, no Stop & Shop. They just had to get off in the woods in the November cold & say "This is home." I don't think I would have had the courage to pick up everything, leave all my family & friends, get in a creaky, leaky, 100-foot wooden boat & go off into the unknown. So, I drink a toast (tea) to our intrepid ancestors (from every country in the world) who stood on a ship deck and watched everything they knew & loved get smaller & smaller & disappear. I can only imagine the seasickness & hardship these people experienced! Two months!

There is nothing so desperately monotonous as the sea; I no longer wonder at the cruelty of pirates.
James Russell Lowell

IT ISN'T EASY BEING GREEN. Going back to bed ...

MAL de MER

HEART IS WHAT DETERMINES OUR FATE. ♥ Isabel Allende

REMEMBER, IT'S ALWAYS DARKEST BEFORE IT TURNS TOTALLY BLACK. SEASICKNESS IS A VERY UNCOMFORTABLE FEELING... TRY NOT TO GET IT...

A Few Helpful Tips...

MAYFLOWER

THE ART OF THE SAILOR IS TO LEAVE NOTHING TO CHANCE. ♥ ANNIE VAN DE WIELE

1. Some people get seasick, but not everyone. Don't let the fear of it stop you. A SHIP IN PORT IS SAFE; BUT THAT IS NOT WHAT SHIPS ARE BUILT FOR. ♥ Grace Hopper

2. Plan how to handle the possibility ahead of time. Once you feel sick, it's already too late. Sad, but true.

3. Good thing about seasickness: it makes you sleepy. Go to sleep.

4. Get fresh air: a few deep breaths, in through your nose, out through your mouth. Don't look at the bobbing horizon!

5. I ♥ acupressure wrist bands. They have a built-in button that sits on pressure points on your wrists for nausea relief. Put them on BEFORE you board the ship.
   A word to the wise

6. Ginger helps; ginger cookies & candy; drink ginger ale.

May 7, cont.
LATER: Noonish   Feeling much better! Moved from our cabin on Deck Eleven, down to more stable Chart Room (Deck Three, mid-ship) to wait for lunch. There's a beautiful rainbow outside! Noon whistle just now: then xylophone tones: bing-bing-bong: "This is the Captain speaking; we just passed the half-way mark on our crossing to Southampton! Weather is clearing: smooth sailing ahead." SWEET MUSIC TO MY EARS!

Joe ordered a Pimm's Cup,* I'm having something new that the waiter suggested: sparkling pear cider over ice. He described it as a "lighter, sweeter beer." He's right, it's delicious! Not too sweet, clean tasting, like champagne that actually tastes good. (I know, blasphemy, right?) It's definitely my new favorite: Joe likes it, too. I'm writing it down, "MAGNER'S PEAR CIDER"... remember that name. ☺ Made in Ireland

PIMM'S CUP ★

And the dreams that you dare to dream really Do Come TRUE...

THE WEATHER CHANGES CONSTANTLY WHEN YOU'RE ON A SHIP; THE SKY, CLOUDS, & COLORS FLY BY, LIKE A TIME-LAPSE VIDEO.

Being here is like being in a Broadway play. We have the BEST ROLES; we get to play "passengers"! It's our job to dress up at night, go dancing, eat, sleep a lot, & indulge ourselves. Others are chefs (with chef-hat costumes); hairdressers & masseuses (they wear nurse costumes & have more technical parts); entertainers (doing double-duty by playing within the play). There are "officers" in white uniforms with gold braid; the most distinguished one plays "the lead," he's "the Captain." I'd be in the program as "seasick passenger" & get a Tony for excellent performance "So REAL," scream the papers). ☺ This gorgeous lit-up ship is our set & there are many costume changes for passengers. Any minute, I expect Fred Astaire to come dancing into the scene, wearing top hat & tails.

Later...AFTER DINNER BEDTIME...

I must have my sea legs! Lunch was good — took a nap, read my wonderful book, did a few sketches for this diary; got my hair cut this afternoon. After dinner, we stopped in to the Queen's Room for a whirl around the dance floor, with a real orchestra. It's old-time glamour straight out of black-&-white movies.

This is a fine romance

Now... back to bed I go. What else can I tell you? This is life around here!

May 8 • Tuesday • 8:30 am

Now this is more like it!

Gorgeous Outside Walked nine times around ship (3.3 mi.), under the life boats that hang above the Promenade Deck (22, btw). Walking in the same direction the ship is going feels like being on one of those people conveyor belts at the airport. *FAST!* Big breaths of salty sea air, sparkling ocean, pristine sky, streaming clouds. There was a girl meditating on the back of the ship, feet up, eyes closed, face to the sun; so I did it, too. Long, wide track of frothy turbulence behind us; pool gently sloshing back & forth in time with the ocean liner; cool wind blowing.

May 8 - Tues.

Back in stateroom now; Joe's up; the door to the deck is open. WHOOSHHH is the sound from outside; bed is covered in wind-ruffled maps of England. I had emails from both Rachel & Siobhan ("Shi-von") — our British friends: they're both coming to see us when we get settled & we'll be staying a few days with each of them, too.

From our deck

Joe just tossed me the Daily Programme; "What do you want to do today?" he asked. (I want to take my book back outside & read!)

Combining reading with staring at sea

"They have a lecture called 'How the Atlantic Ocean Was Formed,'" he said, enthusiastically. (He would probably have to go to that one) Luckily, there are many other choices: "Martini Mixology", Movie class, poker lessons, ball-room dancing, scarf tying, *...On a day like today...* Hostess Corner Knitting", a fruit and veggie-carving demonstration; & the movie today is *The Artist.* But I fear we will do what comes naturally: go somewhere with our books & stare at the sea, zombie-mesmerized by unending view, until naptime!

LOVE the book I'm reading, *Elizabeth and Her German Garden.* It's a semi-auto-biographical novel by Elizabeth von Arnim (born in Australia, grew up in England). Despite what you read here in this diary, my days are actually spent having tea with her among the roses & bees in her most wonderful garden. She refers to her domineering husband as "Man of Wrath," & every time she writes about him, I laugh out loud. Eccentric, charming, witty; so smart, she is. Published in 1898 and still perfect in 2012! It was her first book! I'm forcing myself to read slowly; I already don't want it to end.

     X...Bye...

Later May 8. Tues., 11 pm, but when we turn the clock forward (like we do almost every night to catch up to England time), it's actually midnight!

Wonderful day, sat out on the back of the ship; went to the Afternoon Tea Dance (they have one every day at 4 pm), with a live orchestra (playing Big Band music) & every delicious English-Tea-Party thing: egg salad, cucumber, & watercress sand-wiches, lemon-thyme scones, Victoria sponge, cream puffs, lavender biscuits. There were real ball-room dancers sharing the floor with the normal

CUNARD

This booklet opens up to a detailed map of the ship; it's how we find our way!

people like us; with straight backs, elbows high, doing that head-snapping thing they do. Sat with a darling young couple from Scotland, 26-year-olds; "Colin" is a policeman & "Fiona" works in the Water Department in Inverness, where they live. They had the cutest accents! Fun hearing about life in other countries; we need to visit Inverness some day, it sounds lovely. ♥

Afterwards we went back to the cabin to dress for dinner; the sea has been calm, but I adjusted my battleship-gray, fashion-coup-de-grâce, inch-wide elastic wrist-bands that I wear all the time now & off we went for Pear Ciders over ice in the Commodore Club. And then to the Captain's Reception in the Queen's Room.

Darling Man getting ready for Captain's Reception

Just had a thought, 💡 they should design these wristbands with a little bling. Black, with sequins; silver & gold; a big sparkly jewel. And flannel ones, for bedtime, like now. goodnight

PETEY

65

Most of us, I suppose, are a little nervous of the sea. No matter what its smiles may be, we doubt its friendship. ♥ H.M. Tomlinson

TOOK THIS PHOTO FROM OUR BALCONY JUST BEFORE SUNRISE THIS MORNING; HUMBLING, PROFOUNDLY BEAUTIFUL.

May 9   Wednesday   7AM
Out there? BIG. Gorgeous. Cold, raw-ocean smell; only thing between me & awe-inspiring foreverness was one good gust of wind! In here? Cocoon life: cozy, quiet, knitting, BBC on Telly; pancakes dripping in maple syrup; English bacon. HAPPY. Going to exercis

Later 3PM In Chart Room: Joe, reading; me, catching up with diary. Went to Golden Lion for lunch, QM2 version of an English pub; watched people playing darts while we ate fish & hips (Joe) & cottage pie (me), with *pear ciders* while filling out our Immigration papers.

Wandered around ship after lunch; stopped at urser's Office to exchange dollars for British pounds. Ve found a show, just starting at the Planetarium on eck Three. Huge, domed auditorium, comfortable chairs ou can lean back in, which I did, thinking, "Uh-oh, is is way too comfortable; pear cider, lunch, sea air, & gently rocking boat = total sleep inducer — how much this show will I see? Oh well," schmooshing deeper my seat, "Joe will like it. Hope I won't snore!"

The room dimmed pink, like sunset; then spots of light began to appear in the "sky," until it was dark as a moonless night and pinpointed with a million "stars,"

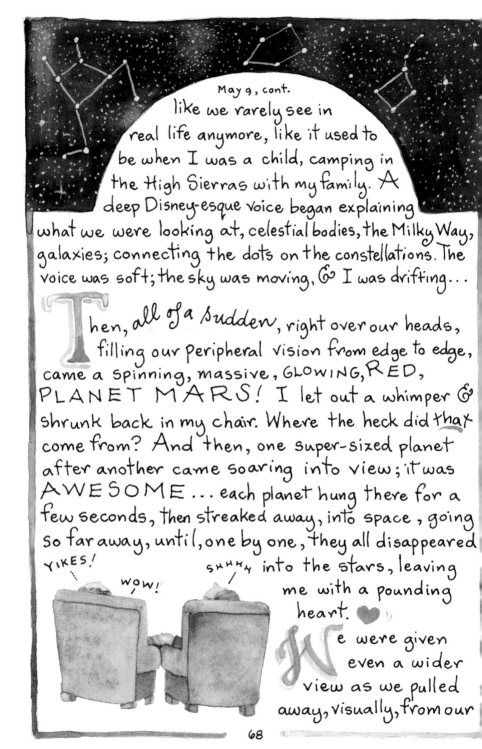

May 9, cont.

like we rarely see in real life anymore, like it used to be when I was a child, camping in the High Sierras with my family. A deep Disney-esque voice began explaining what we were looking at, celestial bodies, the Milky Way, galaxies; connecting the dots on the constellations. The voice was soft; the sky was moving, & I was drifting...

Then, all of a sudden, right over our heads, filling our peripheral vision from edge to edge, came a spinning, massive, GLOWING, RED, PLANET MARS! I let out a whimper & shrunk back in my chair. Where the heck did that come from? And then, one super-sized planet after another came soaring into view; it was AWESOME... each planet hung there for a few seconds, then streaked away, into space, going so far away, until, one by one, they all disappeared

YIKES!

WOW!

SHHHH

into the stars, leaving me with a pounding heart. ♥

We were given even a wider view as we pulled away, visually, from our ur own Solar System, all the planets were orbiting around the Sun, the way we usually see them. Our Sun isn't a big star when compared to others... it's "average-sized," but it's a million times bigger than Earth.

As we got farther away, the Solar System receded in size; the planets became so tiny, they were no longer visible; the light of the Sun faded, became just a pin-prick, mixing with billions of other stars, until we couldn't see it at all! And our sweet little blue-green Earth (with the teensy ocean liner on it)? Gone, too... lost in the enormity of the Cosmos.

For a few seconds, the theater stayed dark, we continued to drift quietly among the stars; then slowly, the light came up, & it was time to go. "We're the drama queens of the Universe," I mumbled to Joe.

This morning, barefooted on our balcony, I was hanging onto the rail, buffeted by the wind, having trouble seeing the exact place where the sea ended & the sky began; I was thinking how big the ship was, how immense the ocean, how staggeringly beautiful, & how lonely it is out there. What a gift our life is, here on Earth, & so often taken for granted. It's good to be reminded of how fragile it all is; just a wobbly thing. If you ever think you need to be put in your place, a planetarium on an ocean voyage is a really good spot to do it!

EXCUSE ME WHILE I KISS THE SKY.

New Rules

1. Don't take things so seriously.

2. Have more fun.

3. Be brave.

Take deep breaths of marvelous Earth atmosphere.

4. Be spontaneous: go places where something pleasantly unexpected can happen to you.

5. Watch more sunrises & sunsets; wish on moon.

6. Don't complain about the weather.

7. Count your lucky stars.

8. Fill heart with beauty.

9. Go on more picnics.

NETTLE-
LEAVED
BELLFLOWER

10. Pick more wildflowers (learn their names!)

11. Slow down time by using some to do nothing.

12. As English poet Rupert Brooke suggested:

FLING SELF ON WINDY HILL, LAUGH IN SUN,
KISS LOVELY GRASS

BEATRIX

4pm BACK IN THE COCOON...

Room service just brought me hot chocolate in a huge cup; I'm mooshed into sofa, wrapped in my green shawl, & MISS POTTER* is on TV! I LOVE THIS MOVIE! I CAN'T BELIEVE IT'S ON IN HERE! When Beatrix dances with Norman Warne while he sings, "When you taught me how to dance"? When Peter Rabbit comes alive? The way it starts, the brush swirling in the watercolors? HEAVEN!

I'm so excited to go to the Lake District to see HILL TOP, the farm Beatrix Potter loved (& left, open to the public, just as it looked in 1943, the day she died)! I've wanted to go for so long; have even been a little afraid to go — it's taking a big chance to give up a beautiful dream for who-knows-WHAT-kind of reality. But we have to go! My life can't go on without it — (must follow Rule #3)!

I've had girlfriends who've made the trip, but I don't let them tell me anything about it. I close my eyes, put my hands over my ears & go la-la-la-la-la la-la-la-la-la until they stop talking.

I took a picture of the TV...

71

I don't want to know. I don't Google her. I want to see it all for the first time with just me & Joe. I don't want to be disappointed by expectations or anyone else's perceptions. I err on the side of caution

When I was in my twenties, I fell in love with the little Beatrix Potter figurines made in Beswick, England, & saved my money to buy them. They've been lined up on a shelf in every kitchen I've ever had. Later on, I read her life story & found out she was a late bloomer, just like me; she believed in fairies, & me, too; her entire life changed when she was in her late thirties; me, too! She survived heartbreak, me, too; she moved far from home to start a new life, bought a small cottage & became house-crazy in the country-place she loved, and I did that too. Books changed both our lives forever. Me & HER? We're like THAT!

NOW I GET TO GO SEE HER HOUSE!

I'm so hoping I find her spirit, alive & well & living at HILL TOP, although, she died only four years before I was born, so a secret part of me believes her spirit might be alive & well & living in ME! TELL NO ONE. I SAID TH

Wed. May 9, cont. from Cocoon...

At one time Beatrix wrote that she saw herself as one of Jane Austen's heroines, so maybe she knew one of my favorite Jane Austen quotes:

IF ADVENTURES DO NOT BEFALL A YOUNG LADY IN HER OWN VILLAGE, SHE MUST SEEK THEM ABROAD. ♥

RULE number 13: Thou Shalt SEEK ☑

And guess what else? We're going to Jane Austen's house too!

THIS IS THE TRIP of HEROES. ♥

Did I write enough today? Oh, I think I did! Going to read my ELIZABETH Book now. Foghorn blowing, dinner later, bed after that.

Tomorrow is our last full day at sea ~~~~ we arrive in ENGLAND Friday morning!

LIFE IS GOOD! Goodnight xoxo for now

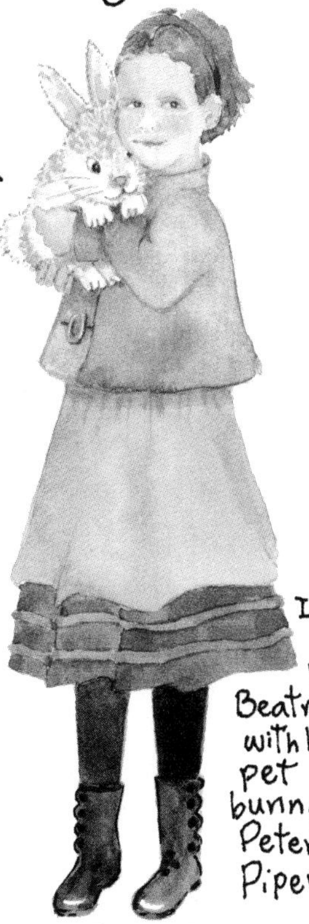

I had to paint Beatrix with her pet bunny, Peter Piper. ♥

May 10, Thursday 10 AM
News from the Cruise
(I KNOW IT'S NOT A CRUISE!)

Last day, dawned clear, fair wind, hazy sea. Went for a long walk to take photos.

Started pulling suitcases out of hiding places; it all needs to be packed up & in the hall outside our door by midnight. We dock in Southampton at 6 AM tomorrow! Joe's piled up all the Cunard chocolates we found under our pillows every night & all the little jars of jam that were on the breakfast tray every morning — packing them up! Organizing art supplies, knitting, books, maps, passports, computer things &

BON VOYAGE

banner &, of course, PETEY, the Sailor man.

I have to write down a quote from my ELIZABETH BOOK ~ it's so adorable. Remember, this is a semi-autobiographical novel & was written in 1898 when

women just had no right to anything. But Elizabeth von Arnim (the author) was very much a thinking woman who uses her novel to espouse her "modern" views. Anyway, to set the scene for this quote: Elizabeth & her visiting girlfriend, Irais, are at Elizabeth's house (with the wonderful garden). Elizabeth's oldest friend has written to ask if her daughter, an art student named Minora (someone E. has not met), can come for a visit. This young woman has all kinds of wildness in her as we can plainly see when she shows up on a BICYCLE! I MEAN, REALLY!

Here's the passage I love — the "I" here is Elizabeth, who speaks to Minora upon arrival, & then rushes to the room of her friend Irais:

"My dear," I said breathlessly to Irais, when I got to her room and shut the door and Minora was safely in hers, "what do you think — she writes books!"

"What — the bicycling girl?"

"Yes, — Minora — imagine it!"

We stood and looked at each other with awestruck faces.

"How dreadful," murmured Irais.

I know it took longer to set up than to say, but I just love this little exchange. So 1898! And yet, look at the brave REAL Elizabeth, nothing is stopping her, not even the awestruck faces around her. I had to laugh — just before we left I got an email from my best friend Diana (in California); her seven-year-old grand-

✱ daughter had called to inform her (using these exact words), "I'm co-authoring a book with one of my friends; I need to find a publisher." Things have changed!

SHE KNEW EXACTLY WHAT SHE WANTED OUT OF LIFE, WHICH, IN A WORD, WAS EVERYTHING. *Dawn Powell*

Later, Noon, May 10, Thursday

On Commodore Club; went shopping for QM2 souvenirs; stopped at duty-free shop for Chanel N°5; dropped off postcards at Purser's office & now we're about to go to lunch.

PEAR CIDER

ROASTED SHALLOTS

soooo Goood!

We recipe-tested this for two but it would be easy to double or triple the ingredients.

1/2 c. aged balsamic vinegar
1/4 tsp. sugar
6 lg. shallots, peeled & halved
1/2 Tbsp. olive oil
sprinkle of salt
1-2 Tbsp. cream cheese
1 Tbsp. Stilton cheese
1 Tbsp. plain breadcrumbs

Preheat oven to 400°. Heat vinegar & sugar; boil down until syrupy; watch so it doesn't burn; set aside.

In small casserole, combine shallots, olive oil & salt. Roast, uncovered, 40 min.

Cream cheeses together; dab evenly over shallots; sprinkle on breadcrumbs; run under broiler 2-3 min., until golden. Drizzle w/ balsamic reduction & serve. Delicious with lamb chops & sweet potatoes!
★ ★ ★ YUM ★ ★ ★

Have I mentioned how good the food has been? At dinner last night, Joe had roasted shallots with a melted cheese sauce that was so DELICIOUS; we think we figured out what was in it. I'm leaving space on this page for it ↑; if it turns out good, I'll put it there; otherwise, more photos! Bye for now

76

Later

Interrupted packing a minute ago to step out on the balcony to look at the sea & suddenly, a big white seagull, the first bird I've seen in six days, came swooping in at eye level, flapping his wings, going the same speed as the ship; just me & him, sailing along with the breeze. We're getting near land! We're underneath Ireland now; he must be an Irish seagull!

Later AFTER DINNER

Everyone saying GOODBYE tonight, exchanging addresses, taking pictures. Passengers gathered up & down on the two curving stair-cases leading to the Grand Lobby — for a SING-A-LONG... *and old songs...*

♪ *It's a long way to Tipperary...* ♪

IF THERE'S A MORE ROMANTIC WAY TO TRAVEL I CAN'T IMAGINE WHAT IT CAN BE.

LAND HO!

THE LOOKOUT

Friday
May 11 · 9:30 am

We're here!

Waiting to disembark — but we can see England right outside the dining room windows (where we are right now).

What a gorgeous day!

We bundled up & went out on deck before dawn to see the lights twinkling along the shore of the Isle of Wight. The sunrise silhouetted faraway church spires;

the perfect background for the glide up the waterway. Surprising how quiet it was, just the call of the sea- gulls, soft putt-putt from tugboats. Three long blasts from the whistle; the massive ship rotated into docking position, deck hands threw lines ashore, & the small crowd around us broke into delighted applause; we'd arrived!

Now, we're just sitting here, waiting for them to call our number so we can go find our luggage & get our- selves to the car-rental place.

Later 7pm *What* a day!
But, we made it. Let's see, OK ... we got off the
ship about 10. No customs at all; we filled out our
immigration papers ahead of time, so that part was
really easy. They had
porters to help us with
our bags. Joe had
ordered ahead for a
cab, & it was there
waiting (you never
know how many
twelve bags is until you see it in the eyes of your
cab driver). He, very charmingly (& forgivingly)
loaded everything up & took us to the car-rental
place where we spent an hour filling out papers.
We rented a safe, strong, tank-like Volvo station
wagon that would fit everything; then we sat in
the car another half hour getting organized,
adjusting seats, figuring out the radio/cd and air;
I was making myself at home with the door pocket,
filling it with knitting, diary, Elizabeth book,
camera, emergency chocolate, Petey, while Joe
was learning how the GPS navigational system
worked. We took our time – trying to get
used to the terrifying idea that soon, with
no practice, Joe would be driving on the

May 11, Friday 7pm cont.

wrong side of the road, from the wrong side of the car, with me on his left, for a three-hour trip across a foreign land. Like being inside out & backwards!

Joe looked at me, "Ready? Seat belt on?"

"Ready," I squeaked.

There is a time to laugh & a time not to laugh and this is one of them. ♥ *Inspector Clouseau*

Slowly, bravely, Joe stepped on the gas. I dried my clammy hands on my knees, pulled my lucky shawl around me, reminded myself that if ever there was a time to resist my natural impulse to express my every thought, this would be it; & off we went, heading for our first rental house in Tenterden, Kent.

Down to the end of the street we wobbled; turned the corner at about one-mile-per-hour, crunching gravel, & then, there was no more time to think about it, because *traffic* was coming at us from all directions. Joe hit the gas, we shot forward, I closed my eyes, & we became

DID WE LOOK INTO TAKING THE TRAIN?

DO ME A FAVOR & TRY NOT TO TALK!

80

one with the zooming, flying melée all around us. We were on an 'M' road, a Motorway, the equivalent of a freeway. According to the GPS Lady, this was the way out of Southampton that would get us to where we needed to go.

I started to put on some music; Joe said, "Oh, please don't do that."

"Right. No. Of course not!"

What was I thinking. Much too soon.

We were completely out of our league, especially in the roundabouts, which seemed to come every few hundred yards, often three or four lanes deep, cars crossing in front of each other (backwards from what we're used to); sometimes there's just a painted dot in the middle of the roundabout; you're supposed to know to go around it. Each one was a wild toad ride eliciting involuntary screams (poor Joe, his screaming really must stop). When we accidentally did something right, we laughed nervously, "That was a good one!" Slightly hysterical.

The English accent of the GPS Woman urges us forward,
"At the next roundabout, take the *third* (pronounce it "thed") exit."
Out loud, together, Joe and I count: "one, two, *three*," as grassy fields & other cars blur past us.
"*Take* the exit," she insists. We do as we are told & careen into the third exit with no idea what's next.

Joe asks me, "What's that white zig-zag line over there . . . what does it mean, do you know?"

Looking back, he changes lanes. Swiveling my head, I help him look back.

"No," I said, "I have no idea. Get over! GET OVER!"

"I'm OVER!!"

"You are running me off the road!"

Whose idea was this anyway?

We did this harrowing thing for about an hour before we finally managed to get off onto a smaller, emptier road that wound through the Sussex Downs. Each little Village, with its multitude of roundabouts, & arrows pointing every which way, took hold of our silver car, like a cocktail shaker, & poured us out into more unfamiliar territory.

After a while we came into a town called Pevensey, & decided, if we could find a restaurant, we should take a break & have lunch. We saw the word PUB, with a driveway we could negotiate,
  (me: "Turn! Turn!" him: "I'm turning!")
which was all the recommendation we needed. We parked near a bank of long grass & wild buttercups & sat there for a moment looking at each other, grateful for the silence, grateful to be alive, grateful for both of us, that it wasn't me driving.

"Oh my God", I said, "I'm so proud of you."

"I wonder if they have pear cider in there?" said Joe, getting out of the car & kneeling to kiss the ground.

The Royal Oak Pub was obviously meant to be a neighborhood "home-away-from-home."

It had an organ next to a big fireplace, a floor-to-ceiling wall of paperback books, videos, & board games, a TV, a sunporch overlooking a lawn & garden, comfy arm chairs, lots of wooden tables & chairs, a big square bathroom completely tiled in pink, and, when Joe asked, our server said,

"Oh, aye-suh; Peah Ci-da, we 'ave it."

They had it. He brought it back with fish & chips & homemade tartar sauce to dip everything in & it was GOOD!

"This," said Mr. Pickwick, looking around him, "This is, indeed, COMFORT."
Charles Dickens

Of all delectable islands the Neverland is the snuggest & most compact... not large & sprawling, you know, with tedious distances between one adventure & another, but nicely crammed.

J·M·Barrie

Aylesbury

LONDON

SURREY

Kent
"THE GARDEN OF ENGLAND"

8
12
6

2
1
7
10
9

11
3

Sussex

4
5

APPROX. 60 MI.

N
W✦E
S

PLACES WE'RE VISITING
ON THIS TRIP: 1-8
GOOD PLACES WE SAW
LAST TIME: 9-12

9. Great Dixter
10. Scotney
11. Sheffield Park
12. Chartwell

1. Tenterden
2. Sissinghurst
3. Batemans
4. Charleston
5. Alfriston
6. Hever
7. Smallhythe Place
8. Knole

TENTERDEN

LATER May 11
Friday 7pm
Kent pop. approx. 8,000

We skidded into the ancient market town of Tenterden at around 4pm. This is the village where we'll be staying for the next two weeks. We rented an apartment ✳ over a restaurant on the High Street (what we would call Main St.), a broad, tree-lined shopping street of darling old buildings filled with antique stores, pubs, tea shops, boutiques, a butcher shop, shoe stores, & a Laura Ashley!

Right in the middle of town ↑ is a medieval church which we can see off the back porch of our rental; we can also hear the bells - which is probably true no matter where you are in England.

Went to pick up groceries before meeting our landlady to get the keys; now we're here & settling in - there's a chicken & potatoes roasting in the oven ~ it almost smells like home! OK~ long day; tell you more tomorrow!

85

Good Morning!
saturday
May 12 · 10am

My eyes flew open this morning when I noticed I wasn't rocking ~ We're in England! Ran to the door to put my face outside ~ cold & damp, it smells like raw celery! And spring! Did my exercises; made tea in strange kitchen; took some

VIEW FROM OUR PORCH

upstairs to Joe; unpacking now; trying to get organized. Last night Joe figured out how to deal with the electricity; he hooked up the transformer & adapters we brought along, so our computers are working!

Joe scrambled eggs, & I arranged my paints & art stuff on the dining table in the "lounge" (what we call the

"living room") across from French doors that overlook the High Street. BBC is on TV (which I found out how to access by pressing every button on the clicker until something happened). BBC says it's 12° Celsius outside; and, btw, according to the

scale upstairs, I weigh nine stones! (Stones! Celsius! I need an interpreter!)

CHURCH BELLS ARE RINGING

I called both Siobhan & Rachel this morning; told them we're here ~

86

Ray will drive over tomorrow afternoon & stay until Tuesday morning; Siobhan comes Tuesday night. Oh! And Siobhan says one stone equals 14 lbs. (which can't be right, not after that boat ride/food fest! Nine stones! 14 × 9 = 126! I don't think so, but I'm going for it!)

On the phone, I was telling Rachel about the huge pigeons outside the window that coo nonstop.

She said, "Oh yes, those are wood pigeons; they're everywhere. My mom says their cooing sounds like they're saying, 'My toe hurts Betty.'"

(Ray delivers this in her English accent; the emphasis on the TOE; pronouncing it, "My TOE huts Bet-tee.")

"Just say it," she went on, "in a singingish, high-pitched, Julia-Child voice; you'll see it's true!"

"My Toe huts Bet-tee," I croon, in falsetto, along with the pigeons. It's true!

We're going out now, to explore the town . . .

MY TOE HUTS BET-TEE!

CELSIUS and FAHRENHEIT

I asked my Blog girls; they said to put Celsius into Fahrenheit. "Double the Celsius number & add thirty; so that makes it 54°F!" (Very handy to have a blog - my girls are so smart! If you're reading this, you know who you are! Better than Google!) ♥

87

May 13 ∘ Sunday ∘ 1 pm

Cool sun is shining in & out between clouds, moving shadows through the kitchen windows. I'm baking a small cake ~ it's in the oven. Rachel's coming this afternoon.

Today is Mother's Day. I put a gift box in the mail for my mom before we left home ~ & I called her last night; she was so surprised to be talking to us "from the other side of the WORLD" ("You're calling me from *England?*") she was knitting, watching tennis on TV, waiting for my sister & the twins to arrive. It was so nice to hear her voice ~ she sounded good!

We have one of these in front of our flat. ♥

TELEPHONE

We walked this morning ~ explored the churchyard, read the gravestones, all crooked & sunk into long wet grass ~ the oldest one I saw was 1683 ~ we went past the Vicarage, over the railroad tracks, down a long path over small wooden bridges & rushing streams, meandering through meadow that went on forever. It's still early spring here, chilly, but we wore sweaters & jackets. We stopped at the supermarket on the way home to get cream & a vanilla bean for the cake ~ & now we are smelling the result.

We brought surprises from Martha Vineyard & some QM2 souvenirs for Ray ~ going to get her room ready & then paint until she gets here. Tomorrow we go to

SISSINGHURST!

88

May 14

'Monday 6am

BBC says:
"SHARP SHOWERS
DUE IN THE NORTH"

Good thing we aren't in the north!

Ray & Joe are still sleeping — I'm up because today we're going to one of my favorite places in the world, a very famous garden near here called Sissinghurst.

Last night, when Ray got here, we walked to a pub up the street for "Sunday Roast" — a pub tradition, like Christmas dinner every Sunday: roast beef, Yorkshire pudding, mashed potatoes, peas & roasted carrots. Then home & over knitting, with dishes of cake & sauce (I'll put the recipe in here — so good!), Ray gave us an "England refresher course" on what things mean & how they work; her favorite market (Waitrose), what the white zig-zag lines on the road indicate ★ "Watch for Pedestrians!"), & what laundry soap to buy. We talked about the DIAMOND JUBILEE, the 60th Anniversary of Queen Elizabeth's ascendancy to the throne, and all the events surrounding it. BIG EXCITEMENT!

89

OUR WALK

RACHEL

The official celebration is the first weekend in June but there are flags & bunting draped on buildings all over this town.

Ray just came downstairs chanting, "MY-TOE-HUTS-BET-TEE" ☺ Better get going . . . Later !

Trooping the Colour 1967
1st

Jubilee postage stamp

HOT MILK CAKE
COALS TO NEWCASTLE, BAKING FOR A BAKER ~ BUT SHE LIKED IT!

This is the perfect thing to make when someone you love is coming to visit; plain, old-fashioned & DELICIOUS!

FIRST MAKE THE

Sauce:
1" piece vanilla bean   1/4 c. sugar
2 c. heavy cream

Slit vanilla bean in half lengthwise & scrape seeds into a small saucepan. Stir in cream & bring to a boil. Add sugar, stir well, cool ~ then chill well.

Now for the

Cake:
Preheat oven to 350°

1/2 c. hot milk
1 rounded tsp. butter
2 eggs
1 c. sugar
1 c. flour, divided
1 tsp. baking powder
Pinch of salt
1 tsp. vanilla

Butter an 8" round or square baking pan. Melt butter into hot milk & set aside. Whisk eggs well in med. bowl. Gradually whisk in sugar, beat well. Stir in 1/2 c. of the flour, the baking powder, salt, & vanilla. Stir in other half-cup of flour, then the hot milk/butter mixture.

Pour into cake pan; bake 40-45 minutes, until edges pull away from sides of pan & toothpick comes out clean. Pour the chilled sauce into a dish & put a slice of cake on top. ENJOY!

MAY 14, *Monday*, cont.

Later **H**ere we go! I'm strapped in the back seat of the car—Joe & Ray are putting "Sissinghurst" ✱ into the GPS — Ray is helping Joe drive so I don't have to! We have batteries in cameras, brought rain coats in case sharp showers sneak up on us. Music now playing ... Vera Lynn ...

We'll meet again, don't know where, don't know when... ♩

Later 7:45 pm

Before I tell you about today— which was WONDERFUL — I want to tell you the story of how I learned about

SISSINGHURST

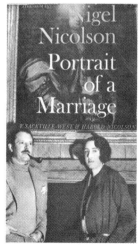

The garden at Sissinghurst is responsible for planting the first seed of "England-yearning" in my heart, all because of a book I read when I was twenty-four called *Portrait of a Marriage*. It was written by Nigel Nicholson, the son of aristocratic parents, Vita Sackville-West & Sir Harold Nicholson. In 1930, Vita & Harold bought the ruins of a 15th-century manor house called

May 14, **monday**, cont.

Sissinghurst, and built wonderful gardens around it.
Portrait of a Marriage alternates chapters taken from Vita's
diary, with chapters written by her son who helped tell the
intriguing story of his parents' unconventional relationship.

IT TAKES COURAGE TO GROW UP AND BECOME WHO
YOU REALLY ARE. ee cummings

Vita loved the country life: flowers, dogs, writing,
art, gardening, traveling ~ but two things from
this book resonated with me & opened doors in my
young & uninformed (to say the least) mind; which was,
at the time, like a hotel with lots of small rooms, but
hardly any furniture ~ only a few knickknacks.

The first thing was that, until then (& I really do hate
to admit this), I believed that everyone pretty much lived
exactly the way we did where I grew up at 13925 Claire
Avenue, Reseda, California, USA. I thought everyone believed
the same things, wanted the same things, read the same
things, & thought the same things were funny. You grew
up, got married, had children, & lived happily ever after.
This was the way life worked. Ask Ozzie & Harriet,
June & Ward Cleaver, Pollyanna's Aunt, or The
Cunninghams. It seemed that's how it was for my parents,

how it would be
for me, & how
it was for
everyone.

But this
couple lived in
a way I'd never
heard of, or
imagined,
& yet, it all
seemed to
work out fine!

92

They were happy (in a "civilized", sophisticated, English blue-blood sort of way); accomplished (she was a writer, he was in gov't. service); had interesting friends (such as Virginia Woolf); children; & made a life that pleased them, on their own terms.

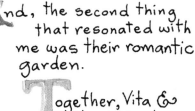

So!, I thought, for the first time, there's more than one path to happiness! I liked that. I thought they were brave. I didn't want to be them, but I liked that *they* wanted to be them. It opened a world of possibilities in my mind, just the idea that everything was much bigger than I thought.

GARDEN
♥
HER ⟷ HIM

And, the second thing that resonated with me was their romantic garden.

Together, Vita & Harold had a passion bigger than themselves, bigger than their marriage, bigger than everything — their garden. No matter what they did during their lives, the legacy they left for generations to come is pure magic. I dreamed of seeing Sissinghurst ever since reading this book.

But at the time, being only twenty-four

and continuing on my path to be a late bloomer, I had a long way to go. First I had to move to the island & meet Joe, fall in love, dream up the dream, & then get the confidence to make it come true.

Finally!

In 2004, on a cool, wet, May mornin' we drove down the long driveway to Sissinghurst for the first time & found ourselves immersed in Harold's & Vita's creativity & dedication.

There were tears in my eyes as I walked the mown path through the tall grass to the wild garden, hearin' the chattering birds, smelling the pink blooms crowding the branches of the old apple trees. It was all real. And a little walk through history.

In the 1300s my blood relative, King Edward I (though we somehow lost touch with the family) stayed the night at Sissinghurst ~ and in 1573, the first Queen Elizabeth (daughter of Henry VIII) spent three nights there.

YOU GOT-TO HAVE A DREAM
IF YOU DON'T HAVE A DREAM
How YA GON-NA MAKE A DREAM COME TRUE?

HAPPY TALK

94

Today, we were just three of the millions of people who've traveled from all over the world to see Sissinghurst; they've had garden visitors since 1937 when Vita charged a shilling for entry. It was just as lovely today as the first time we saw it, only this time we got to see it with Rachel!

The garden is divided into flower-scented "rooms" with arched doorways, brick walls dripping with pink clematis, & high, clipped hedges. You come through a door or an opening in a hedge & "discover" the moat walk, the rose garden, the cottage garden (filled with spring flowers), the famous White Garden (where you melt when you see the stone love seat planted in chamomile), the herb garden, the yew walk, & the gazebo. ♡

Garden Rooms Viewed from Tower

The three of us climbed the Castle Tower for a windy birds-eye view of the garden rooms, as clearly marked as the rooms in a doll house, furnished in plants.

CLEMATIS "MONTANA"

Vita's writing room is in the Tower, halfway up the curving staircase; her books, framed photographs, paintings, & her writing desk, all as she left them.

It's Sleeping Beauty's Castle. ♥ Vita Sackville-West

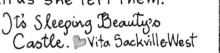

HELP! I'M MELTING...

There's a plant shop at Sissinghurst, a gift shop & a a TEA ROOM — with a long view across meadows & woodlands, flitted over by songbirds, divided by hedgerows & dotted with lambs.

We've now seen the garden twice, both times too early for the White Garden to be in bloom. So, at the

THE WHITE GARDEN, "BEFORE."

end of June, just before we get on the ship to go home, we're coming back! We can't go without seeing the roses. (You can come too, we're all in this together.)

"WE ARE THE DAY, THE NIGHT, THE LIGHT, THE DARK, THE WATER DROP, THE STREAM; THE MEADOW, THE LARK."
VITA SACKVILLE-WEST

We got back to the car just as it began to rain & drove through the winding hedgerows to a nearby pub that Rachel found with her cell phone. (We brake for "circa 1420!")

The pub was a maze of cozy dark rooms in wood & brick, low ceilings, wide-planked floors, heavy, hand-hewn beams & a fire burning in every room. Old books lined the walls;

THE THREE CHIMNEYS
FREE HOUSE
circa 1420

96

there were mismatched chairs, benches & tables, & bunches of hops hung from the beams. It smelled like centuries of wood fires & cooking food (in a good way!). From the chalk-board menu, I ordered smoked haddock with leeks in cream sauce & Parmesan-roasted potatoes, & washed it all down, along with the cares of the day (not that there were any!), with Pear Cider.

We drifted through the afternoon, three good friends who love to cook; talking & sharing bites of everything: butternut squash, fish cakes, broccoli soup, & creamed leeks; ordering hot rhubarb cobbler for dessert & having tea.

Rain pattering the windows, popping embers, the hum of voices, chairs scraping on wood; so cozy & old & filled with ghosts; historical, wonderful ghosts. Vita & Harold, in muddy boots & rough coats might have been seated right where we were. Maybe Vita & Virginia Woolf. Why not?

The country habit has me by the heart.
Vita Sackville-West
(M E, Too)

Now, the happy ending. We are home; Ray is curled in the yellow chair reading *A Room of One's Own* (by V. Woolf) she got today at the gift shop. Joe is on the sofa with a book about hedges & I'm writing. DOMESTIC BLISS ♥ (Good Night)

97

GOING BACK IN TIME THROUGH THE
HEDGEROWS

'd heard the word, but not until I came to England did I understand what it meant. "Hedgerow" is what British people call any hedge; but because England is so old, mixed hedges were planted, beginning a thousand years ago, not decoratively, but to make boundaries & enclose farm-lands & pastures. Rural roads are almost always bordered by a hedgerow or a stone wall, or both. Many hedgerows are now protected; not only are they beautiful, they're an essential habitat for birds, insects, & small animals. Beneath the hedges, called the "understory," grows all the wild things, bluebells, meadowsweet, common mallow, oxeye daisy, primrose, & buttercups, to name a few. To me, hedgerows are a national treasure & part of the reason our own national treasure, Mark Twain, was inspired to say:

RURAL ENGLAND IS TOO BEAUTIFUL TO BE LEFT OUT of DOORS.

May 15,
Tuesday 3 pm

Dark; raining ~ I'm at the art table, painting rain ~ We took the day off, staying in, writing, reading, doing laundry. Ray left this morning, but we'll see her & Paul (her husband) on our way north to the Lake District, so it wasn't a true goodbye. 💙 She had something like ten trays of brownies to make by this after- noon! She was telling us last night that her great-great-grandfather opened his first bakery in 1866, so that makes her a 4th-generation baker!

And now, our other English friend, Siobhan, is on her way; should be here any minute. Tomorrow we're going with her to visit two houses ~ one is BATEMAN'S, the home of Rudyard Kipling, & the other is a house Siobhan thinks we will love, called CHARLESTON, which was owned at one time by Virginia Woolf's artist sister, Vanessa, whom I never heard of, but Siobhan is crazy about her art & style.

This funny thing hangs over the sink in the bathroom here ~ there's a magnet mashed into the soap ~ that's what's holding it on!

What so many of the houses we're touring have in common, including Sissinghurst, Beatrix Potter's 'Hilltop,' & Bateman's, is that they're all owned by an amazing British charity called...

The National Trust*

Since 1895, the NATIONAL TRUST has been preserving open spaces & rescuing hundreds of historical properties in England, Wales, & Northern Ireland, from as far back as the 14th century; ranging from the opulent to the quirky to the humble; castles, country homes, farms, cottages, windmills, dovecotes, medieval churches, pubs, & even whole villages. They've been restored with the help of traditional craftspeople & artisans & opened to the public.

We are card-carrying members of the Royal Oak Society,* which entitles us to free admission to National Trust properties. At many of the properties, there are lovely tea rooms & gift shops; everything is run by local volunteers who share their passion for the places they help care for. We keep a National Trust map in the car, so wherever we are, we know what properties are near us. There is SO much to learn in every one of them!

Eight years ago, the last time we came to England (with Sissinghurst as our inspiration), wishing to have a purpose to our travel, we followed our map over hill & dale, through small country villages & visited twenty-five houses, castles, & gardens. What we learned was that there is much more

100

to see in this country than Big Ben & Buckingham Palace. In rural England, these preserved architectural treasures and the revealing glimpses into the lives of the people who lived and worked in them, wove intimate human stories that made history come alive for us, touched our hearts & imaginations.

Joe was skeptical the first time we came; he wasn't so sure he would love going to a "bunch of gardens." But these were gardens like we'd never seen before, & every one of them came with a house, & every house had a story of lives led there, and every day we gasped at the beauty of what we were seeing. It absolutely never got old, and Joe was as thrilled with it as I was — and he still is, and I still am, so here we are again!

God gave all men all earth
to love,
but since our hearts are
small,
ordained for each, one spot
should prove
beloved over all.

RUDYARD KIPLING

Wouldn't you LOVE to see the "beloved spot" that inspired this poem?
OK! That's where we're going next!

BATEMAN'S*

H♥ME of RUDYARD KIPLING

May 17, Thursday
2 pm

I'm having tea, writing in my diary in a little tearoom downtown — Joe went to Ashford, looking for a hardware store.

on the counter...

Gorgeous day yesterday: good weather, blue skies; two houses & a darling town. Siobhan got here Tuesday night; yesterday morning we were up early & on the road...first stop?

Bateman's

I knew almost nothing about Rudyard Kipling before we went to his home near the tiny village of Burwash. I knew he was famous for writing the *Jungle Book*, & that his hero, growing up, was Mark Twain, whom he longed to meet, & DID in a "predestined" sort of way, while traveling through America when he was twenty-four & still unknown. Mark Twain wrote a wonderful story about this meeting & their subsequent friendship in his autobiography — & that was all I knew!

Kipling* bought Bateman's in 1902, then wrote:

Behold us, lawful owners of a grey-stoned lichened house — "A.D.1634" over the door — beamed, paneled, with old oak staircase; & all untouched & unfaked. ♥ RUDYARD KIPLING 1865-1936

The place is like a little fiefdom, a miniature kingdom, with all the things the big castles have: mullioned windows, oak beams, formal gardens — but it's also a family home. His study was lined in books, including a worn copy of *Little Women*. His typewriter & glasses were there. There were Victorian toys in the nursery. I stood in the same room with his 1907 Nobel Prize for Literature! Thrilling! 1907 had to be a red-letter year for Kipling; it's also the year he & Mark Twain (thirty years his senior) were awarded honorary degrees from Oxford in a ceremony together (these two boys who quit formal schooling while in their teens).

About Kipling, whom he much admired, Mark Twain wrote,

HE IS A MOST REMARKABLE MAN; BETWEEN US WE COVER ALL KNOWLEDGE; HE KNOWS ALL THERE IS TO KNOW, & I KNOW THE REST.

FLOWER OF THE DAY WAS EVERYWHERE

FORGET-ME-NOT

May 17, cont.

Kipling used his Nobel Prize money to design & build his beautiful garden. After we toured the house, we went outside to smell the wisteria, clematis, bluebells, & forget-me-nots: we wandered along the yew hedges, into the rose garden, through the apple orchard — there's a lovely pond, a wildflower-banked river with a wooden bridge, a working flour mill & a tearoom amongst the fruit trees.

Kipling had a cow named BUTTERPAT (right there, I could fall in love with him!).

His wife, Carrie, was an American from Vermont. I found a book about her in the gift shop, written by Adam Nicholson, the grand son of Vita Sackville-We (Everything is connected around here!) Carrie Kipli died in 1939, leaving the hous & contents (furnished jus as they left it) to the National Trust. THANK YOU CARRIE

— SIOBHAN —

The server in here just told me I have a cute accent! She doesn't know it, but she's the one with the cute accent!

Pardon me one moment while I take a bite of of this delectable little cucumber sandwich. Mmmmm. I can see the church outside the window & hear the bells. Where am I? This must be a D R E A M.

Before we left Bateman's, we had tea & Lemon Cake at a table among the flowering apple trees, & then, it was time to go on to our next stop: Charleston.

Joe, & our darling friend SIOBHAN, mapped our course through the hedgerows lined with cow parsley & overhung with hawthorn. Just like going through the wardrobe — when we emerge on the other side, we will be somewhere we've never been before in a land time forgot, at a house Siobhan told us about, an amazing house with artistic history & personality called Charleston, near Lewes, in East Sussex.

As formal, paneled, & dark as Bateman's was, Charleston was the opposite; not a house built with money — a house built with HEART. ♥

The rooms & furnishings were homemade, WHIMSICAL,

Music playing is FRANK: FLY ME to the MOON ♪

105

CHARLESTON

May 17, cont.

VANESSA

VIRGINIA

and charming, decorated in the style called "Arts & Crafts" (which I'd heard of, but I always associated it with Frank Lloyd Wright & Stickley furniture; styles I've never been attracted to ~ but, apparently, as I've been learning, there is more to it). This house was more interesting than I ever imagined — I loved it!

HERSTORY:

Charleston was the home of Vanessa Bell (b.1879) who was the sister of Virginia Woolf (b. 1882).

A bit of history in a nutshell: Vanessa & Virginia were very close. They suffered from abuse when young, & depression as they got older; Virginia especially: on March 28,1941, she put on her overcoat, filled the pockets with stones, walked into the river near her home, & drowned herself; Vanessa died of natural causes & was buried April 12, 1961 (on my fourteenth birthday).

The two accomplished artists supported the suffragette movement, were pacifists, & the center of an influential group of writers, intellectuals, philosophers & artists called The Bloomsbury Group (Vita Sackville-West, because of her relationship with Virginia, was on the fringes of this group). Defying convention was a

106

by Vanessa Bell

FOR MOST of HISTORY, "ANONYMOUS" WAS A WOMAN. *Virginia Woolf*

large part of who they were; the Victorian age was over; they were young & they wanted to change the world. The relatively bohemian lives they chose for themselves were very much outside the box of "normalcy" at the time. They bravely determined to live their lives on their own terms & damn the torpedos.

In 1916, Virginia told Vanessa about a house she'd found for lease, very near her own. Vanessa took it, along with her partner, the artist Duncan Grant, & Charleston became the country gathering place for their artistic friends & extended family, including E.M. Forster (who wrote *A Room with a View* & *Howards End* ~ wonderful books if you haven't read them ~ &, incidentally he was also the tutor to Elizabeth von Arnim's children ~ the woman who wrote the book I just finished, *Elizabeth and her German Garden!* See? I told you, they're all connected!).

THEN WE GOT TO TOUR THE HOUSE!

Here's what we found: What Vanessa & Duncan did besides creating wonderful paintings, filled with light & color, was to imaginatively,

May 17, cont.

charmingly, hand-paint or
stencil every single corner
of this house, around all
the fireplaces, all the bookcases, the walls, doors, floors,
even the chairs & tables
(which were a mish-mash
of furniture styles & periods;
some of the pieces looked
like they'd been found on
the side of the road). They
designed & made pottery &
tiles, & colorful, modern

fabrics in simple patterns they used to
cover the furniture, drape on beds, &
make curtains. They did needlepoint
to die for, painted lamp shades, hung their
paintings on the walls, & the whole thing
came together in what I would describe
as whimsical, sophisticated elegance; the MOST
handmade house I've ever seen! They didn't have
money, so they made things. Can't afford wallpaper? No problem, paint
it on!

Time has faded the
colors a little,
but it was easy to
"see" it as it used to
be, vibrant and
new. If this is
ARTS & CRAFTS,
then count me in!

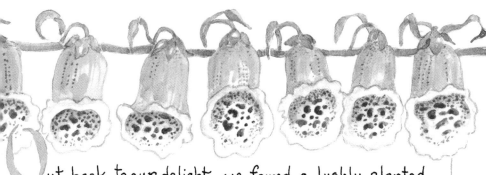

Out back, to our delight, we found a lushly planted walled garden where we were allowed to wander to our heart's content. There were paths & benches

wreathed in forget-me-nots & a blackbird sang in an apple tree. There were roses climbing over windows and doors; we can only imagine what this garden will look like in the summer when it's in full bloom. Even now, next to the front door there's a border that looks like it came right out of a crayon box, the same riot of color that seems to be the hallmark of this house. ♥

Nothing is more the child of art than a garden.

Sir Walter Scott

May 17, cont.

Next to the house was a wonderful tea room with a bouquet of garden flowers on the counter, next to a jug of cream from the local dairy. Powder-blue painted walls, rose-patterned oilcloths on the tables; they served the tea in Emma Bridgewater mugs! We tasted Rose Lemonade & Shandy, which is beer mixed with lemonade. I had a grilled brie sandwich with heirloom tomatoes & basil pesto on crunchy brown toasted bread; licked dripping cheese off edge of crust—I wrote it down while we were there so I can make it later!

The guide in the house had mentioned a nearby church where Vanessa & Duncan had painted the interior in the 1940s, so that's where we went next. The inside of the church was interesting, but the outside was a painting come alive!

As I walked up the steps, I looked back & my heart did a little back-flip ~ the view! I felt like I'd been there before, with the bluebells & trilling birds; the breeze through the trees, the mooing cows, the cottage beyond the hedge, & pigeons crooning "My toe huts Bet-tee!"

I don't think I'll be getting over Charleston very soon; the stories of the people, the house; they were so REAL ~ like reading a really good book you can't quit thinking about.

Note to Sue: When you get home, remember to give a corner of the house the Charleston, Arts & Crafts, Bloomsbury look: find the equivalent of bright English meadow flowers; stuff them into a jam jar or jug (English for pitcher, & best chipped). Set the jug on top of a pile of old books, & voila ~ squint your eyes ~ you're bohemian, romantic, suffragette. brave writer ~ artist. ♥

ALFRISTON

Such a cute town — must come back!

Siobhan left us there; it was time for her to head back to her home in Gloucestershire. We hugged good-bye, knowing we'll be going to stay with her & her husband, John, toward the end of the trip. Off she went & off we went.

We wanted to go to Monk's House, where Virginia Woolf lived — it was so near — but it was closed by the time we got going; instead we went looking for a special book-store we'd heard about in the ancient village

MUCH ADO BOOKS
New & Old Books for all Readers & Collectors

of Alfriston — but the bookstore was closed, too. I knew the day was officially over when we finally sat down in front of a fire in the George Inn Pub (1397!) and I told Joe my "eggs were laking." And that's BEFORE the pear cider. (Say it out loud.)

OK, that's it; we're all caught up. I've finished the last drop of tea, the last crumb of scone. Joe should be back soon. I'm walking to the grocery store to get some Rose Lemonade, brie, bread, tomatoes, & organic granola Ray told me about — And there's an antique store on the way home! Byeee!

THE GEORGE INN

On the Street where we live...

WALKING THROUGH TOWN

WE ♥ WAITROSE GROCERY STORE ~ THEY WEAR UNIFORMS!

LOOK at the book I found at the antique store!

WHOLE TOWN IS DECORATED FOR THE JUBILEE - FLAGS & BUNTING!

The Flower Shop

THESE 45s FOR SALE AT THE THRIFT STORE

DOES ENCHANTMENT POUR OUT OF EVERY DOOR

CAN YOU HEAR A LARK IN ANY OTHER PART OF TOWN

ONLY HERE ON THE STREET WHERE WE LIVE

A ROSE-COVERED COTTAGE WAITS for you.

THEY CALL A REALLY DARLING COTTAGE

"A Box of Chocolates"

There are many choices for places to stay in England, everything from five-star hotels, to quaint bed & breakfasts, rooms in castles, cozy country house hotels, or downtown flats. We usually rent a house or a flat so we have our own kitchen & a place to call "home." There are many nice houses in every part of the country, but the rose-covered cottages & "chocolate boxes" do go first! It's easy to find rentals online — just Google "vacation rentals in England" for virtual tours galore!

Some things you should ask about:

Do you want WiFi? Or a garden? Is a bathtub OK, or would you like a shower? Is there a washer and dryer? How close is your parking place to your rental? Would you want a fireplace? (It's often drizzly in England; after a long day of garden walking, coming home to a cup of tea in front of a wood-fire is a wonderful thing.) Also, if you like to stretch out on the sofa, a good rule of thumb is to look for three cushions on the sofas you'll see in the pictures online. If you only see two, it's probably a love seat. Last, no matter where we've stayed in England, even in hotels, there has always been an electric tea kettle provided. It's very civilized. ♥

JACK

A RING DISH I BOUGHT AT CHARLESTON

GIRL

May 18, Friday 11am

Been shmooshed into the love seat reading my Charleston book, thinking what this rental lacks in cottagy charm (which is total), it makes up for by being comfortable & walking distance to everything. But next time, I'm starting earlier & holding out for cottagy charm! And a garden.

I DO LOVE OUR CHURCH BELLS!

Got an email this morning from Will, the guy staying with our kitties — so sweet of him to send these photos of my babies — I see no recrimination in their eyes!

Feeling inspired by what we've been learning — CHARLESTON & BLOOMS-BURY — so interesting. Been painting borders for my Charleston pages — forgot to bring a pencil sharpener.

HEVER CASTLE*

May 19, Saturday 2 pm

That's ↗ where we are right now — it's Hever Castle, the childhood home of ANNE BOLEYN — doomed wife of Henry VIII, Queen of England for about three years, & mother of Queen Elizabeth I! It's the perfect fairy tale castle, built in

1270, not very big, charming to look at, with a drawbridge & a moat & within "riding distance" (30 mi.) to London. Anne's father inherited it & the family moved in around 1500. Anne's bedroom was little & perfect; you can easily imagine her growing up there (you can imagine your SELF growing up there!) I could picture twelve-year-old Anne, looking out

116

her bedroom window, wishing on stars, dreaming of her romantic future — but over in the corner, invisible to her, but NOT to us, destiny lurks like a spider. (I've had my share of love & loss, but at least it didn't include execution! A few years after he "done her in," Henry gave Hever away to one of his other ex-wives in a divorce settlement!! Insult added to injury!) You can easily picture Henry VIII & his men riding up to the place in their costumes, armed to the teeth, trumpets blowing, horse hooves clattering over the drawbridge — you want to yell, "RUN!"

A N N E B.

Sound the ALARM! Alert the guards! CLOSE the Portcullis!

In 1903, William Waldorf Astor, the richest man in America & a person who LOVED history, bought Hever & spent a fortune restoring it as his family's residence. It's him you see reflected everywhere in the castle now. The rooms are gorgeous, the furniture is comfy looking — I'd LOVE to have a party in the beautiful drawing room! He added lavish, & I mean LAVISH, gardens & created a lake (800 locals dug it — thirty-eight acres, by HAND!) where you can go rowing; people were picnicking on the lawns, under huge trees. It's really wonderful — worth every moment we've spent here.

May 19 Saturday, cont.

There's a border of yellow tulips with orange & purple nemesia all the way around the castle that is so cheerful — I should really start a little garden book to keep track of these ideas! We've taken a million photos — will want proof it wasn't all a dream.

Our cakes are baked daily by Pauline in our Castle Kitchens

Later We're in the tea room here at the castle — there are bluebells in vases on every table. We spent hours walking around the gardens, finding so many things to see — there's a maze! They also have a B&B here. If we'd only known — we could easily spend a few days. I'd love to be here after dark, or walk around the lake at dawn. Or Christmas! With all this history! Can you imagine? With snow, in front of a fire? We have to come back.

TRY THIS AT HOME

— LIKE A WILDFLOWER BORDER —

NEMESIA

SERENGETI SUNSET

YELLOW TULIPS

SERENGETI UPRIGHT PURPLE

Anne's HANDWRITING — I LIKE HER 'A'.

Anne the queue

In short, there's really not
a more congenial spot...
Camelot

Choose your roads wisely & be sure a few of them are dirt.
PUBLIC FOOTPATHS

*O*n Martha's Vineyard, Joe & I have taken the same walk almost every morning for the last twenty years — a brisk exercise walk out a dirt road, through the woods to the sea. It's our favorite part of the day.

*S*o we were ecstatic to learn that behind every small town in England, criss-crossing the country, there are public footpaths, some even hundreds of miles long, that wind across fields & farms, through woods & towns, along rivers & over streams, & through areas of "Outstanding Natural Beauty," ☆ connecting every country village.

*T*hese paths are the same routes that have been

WE MET THIS MAN WALKING WITH HIS DOGS

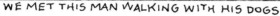

sed since the beginning of time
y people taking their goods to
market, going to church, &
visiting friends for the hundreds,
even thousands, of years before
there were cars. It is possible
to walk across England,
stopping along the way at

pubs & bed and breakfasts, making every day an adventure.

ou can find maps to these walk-routes at
local shops in every region. We use the "OS
EXPLORER MAPS." ⭐ The paths are marked;

you simply walk down an
alley in any village, &
right out of town, amongst
farm animals ⌒ into
    SERENDIPITY;
you never know what you
will find. We have ex-
perienced our best travel
moments by doing this, because nothing is planned;

there are no
expectations; it's
all a surprise.
Turn the page &
I'll show you what
it looks like.

Follow Joe ➔

THE QUEST *for* INSPIRATION OFTEN LEADS TO

COMING?

THOUSAND-YEAR-OLD TREES TURN EVERYONE INTO TREE HUGGERS

We walk in pastures with lambs

FAT CHICKENS

WILD FLOWER MEADOWS & LITTLE COTTAGES

THE DOOR *of* LEARN[illegible]

MORNING, STRETCH & YAWN AND ASK YOURSELF

(BECAUSE YOU REALLY DON'T KNOW), "WHAT SHALL WE DO TODAY?"

HILL & DALE

OVER STILES

AMONGST SHEEP

FOLLOW THE PATH

ACROSS BRIDGES

OVER THE RIVER, THROUGH THE WOODS

 AROUND THE CORNER, THERE MAY WAIT
A WINDING PATH THROUGH A SECRET GATE.

SMALLHYTHE PLACE*

MONDAY, MAY 21 2 PM

I'm at a table on a lawn, in a tea-room garden; across the grass, bees are floating along a wooden fence lined in lacy cow parsley — we're having tea in the sunshine; I'm taking notes for my diary. What started out this morning as a "one-hour exercise walk" turned into something else when we got onto a path that became progressively more charming. To the point that we could not stop!

SHOULD WE GO BACK?

AN UNEXPECTED TURN IN THE ROAD... 💙

We'd already gone through gates, across a field of lambs, into the woods — were getting more excited to ee what was around the next end. We were following a ildflower-strewn path beside river when Joe pulled out s map & said,

"OK, we've been walking for an hour — we can turn back w, or go on... what do you want to do?"

I nodded, "What's up ahead?"

He said, referring to his map, "It looks like ere's a National Trust property in the next town, in out another mile and a half — it's got a house that as once owned by an actress."

The path was calling my name. "It's too beautiful go back!" (birds went tweet-tweet-tweet.)

Joe said, "Let's go on then, but, remember, there are o taxis out here."

I laughed, thinking, *National Trust means tea room o bathroom! I won't need a taxi.*

I'm so glad we didn't go back — the walk was wonderful & the house turned out to be e of the smallest & most arming Nat'l Trust houses we've er seen — definitely a 'Box of ocolates!' I'm in the backyard w — it's a Tudor cottage, →
lt in 1500, purchased in 1899 a famous Victorian stage tress named

ELLEN TERRY.

125

SMALLHYTHE
PLACE

ELLEN LIKED TO HAVE HER TEA AT THIS TABLE IN HER BEDROOM

She used the cottage as a get-away from her busy life in London for almost thirty years. After Ellen died, her daughter Edy (another friend of Vita Sackville-West!) gave the property to the Nat'l Trust, just as it was when her mother was alive.

THE BEAUTIFUL ELLEN TERRY

♥ FORGET-ME-NOT

There wasn't a square angle left in the house — the tilted & bent roof, layered with hand-made clay tiles, set the tone. Inside, creaky wooden floors sloped up & down along the hallway; low ceilings, doors & windows were crooked from old age.

Ellen Terry had every convenience in her London home, but she kept Smallhythe as it was when she found it; no electricity or running water — only candles & oil lamps.

I can just imagine how quiet it was when she was there, with only nature noises & the sound of her own footsteps. Her stage costumes, her jewelry, her sewing box, personal photos, hair combs, a telegram from King George V & memento of her amazing life & career were on display.

SHE ALWAYS KEPT A ROW OF GERANIUMS ON HER WINDOWSILL

ALL WE COULD HEAR WERE BIRDS

Outside, we walked along the grassy paths through Ellen's rose garden, the orchard, all in pink bloom, the nuttery, through the hedge openings (picking buttercups) to the churchyard next door.

The lambs in the field were bleating, the birds were singing; the wind blew through the leaves & across the gravestones; buttercups bent and flowed like a tide in the tall grass, bees ranged through the lilacs & apple blossoms, the clouds broke, the sun came out; the view that goes on forever is old; there is nothing to jar the eye; a few other crooked rooftops are visible above the hedges — that's how it is & has always been, here in this place in beautiful

THROUGH THE 'WILD GARDEN'

"May.

Lay thy shadows on the sundials, & on the meadows, let the winds go loose."

Rainer Maria Rilke

MOUNDS OF FORGET-ME-NOTS SURROUND THE HOUSE ♥

127

Good Morning!

May 22, Tuesday 7 a.m. It's a little overcast out there but BBC says it will clear.

Was just thinking—before yesterday, I never heard of Ellen Terry—but her wonderful cottage garden was overflowing with twinkly blue forget-me-nots — I bet she'd LOVE seeing her picture here, & knowing she's not forgotten. 💙

On the way home from SMALLHYTHE, I asked Joe to lay down in a field of buttercups so I could take his picture. He looked at the meadow & sunshine & said,
   "If I lay down there, I'm not getting up!"
He picked up this woodpecker feather from the path, handed it to me, saying,
   "Put this in your diary."
So there it is — this diary now has English woods-walk woodpecker DNA in it — plus buttercups. Who could ask for anything more?

BBC REPORTS: PRINCE PHILIP CALLS THE QUEEN, HIS WIFE, "LILIBET," "DARLING," OR (and this is the one I'm not so sure about), "SAUSAGE." (PROBABLY SOUNDS BETTER WITH AN ENGLISH ACCENT!)

Eating coconut yogurt with blueberries & granola waiting for Joe to get up so we can go for a walk. Today is Tuesday- time is flying, we start heading north on Friday!

Wood pigeons crooning, "MY-TOE-HUTS-BET-TEE ♫"

May 23, Wednesday 7 pm

Knole*

Today we visited Knole, a 365-room Country House, one of the largest in England. Built around 1465, it's the ancient family home to the aristocratic Sackvilles, & the birthplace of Vita Sackville-West.

Vita was the daughter & only child of the third Lord Sackville; her parents were first cousins, her grandfathers were brothers, but that still didn't make her quite "Sackville enough." She needed to have been born a boy; then she would have inherited Knole; instead the law demanded the estate go to her cousin Eddy. When her father died, Vita had to leave the place she adored, the only home she'd ever known, which she resented, quite rightly, for the rest of her life.

The castle ruin of Sissinghurst was Vita's creative attempt to make up for it. Although there's a vague resemblance between the two houses, Knole is vast and substantial, while Sissinghurst is relatively small & slightly crumbling & has garden rooms instead of real ones.

K N O L E

S I S S I N G H U R S T

May 23, Wednesday, cont.

THE DARK FAIRY TALE TRUE-LIFE STORY of VITA, A TURN-OF-THE CENTURY PRINCESS WHO BROKE ALL THE RULES, RAN AWAY TO PARIS WITH HER LOVER, DISGUISED IN MEN'S CLOTHING.

"A rotten lot, and nearly all stark staring mad." Vita, describing her ancestors. And from what I've read of the fascinating history of the Sackvilles at Knole (from the guide book at the gift shop), she's right! Generations of people who lived their pampered, self-centered lives, smothered in diamonds, embroidered satins & brocades; edged in gold & silver lace, draped in velvet & fur (in addition to marrying relatives) — how could they be normal? They would make the perfect soap opera!

I do like to imagine what the twenty-six-acre walled garden would have looked like if Vita & Harold had gotten their hands on it ⟶ then again, maybe it would be nothing at all; maybe NOT having Knole was her inspiration for Sissinghurst ⟶ guardian angels don't always wear white.

Knole belongs to the Nat'l. Trust now — but the current Lord Sackville & his family (probably very nice people) still live there, over 400 years after the first Sackvilles took residence. The public part of the house is filled with gorgeous 16th-, 17th-, & 18th-century furniture, tapestries & paintings. It's not a house of the heart like Charleston & Smallhythe, but a house of lords & ladies, dukes & duchesses, counts & countesses, kings & queens — filled with history.

Funny, in the 15th century, when Knole was built, it seems almost impossible that they were able to construct something so grand with only primitive tools & yet they did it all the time — even if some buildings took four or five generations to finish — they still did it! England is filled with awe-inspiring castles & cathedrals, made hundreds of years ago, before there were power tools. Funny thing is, now that we can do it so much easier, we don't!

May 24, Thursday 2pm
Leaving "The Garden of England" tomorrow — heading north to BEATRIX POTTER'S, via Rachel & Paul's. Getting ready to go, I was doing laundry, using the 1950s-type clothesline outside our flat — the four-sided kind that turns, & collapses. I put it up, the same way you would a giant umbrella, but got the plastic lines caught under my nose for a moment; then the whole thing came out of the hole & I teetered around in the yard, trying to get it back in, feeling like a ditzy Mary Poppins.

HELP!

I finally got it back in the hole & in the UP position, which I imagined was permanent — so I hung the wet clothes on it, which is when it collapsed again & this time I was inside the lines, amongst the wet clothes, where I staggered around, fighting for my life; I did not want to fall over! — until Joe came out, laughing himself silly, from his view through the kitchen window, & saved me. This would NEVER have happened to any Sackvilles!

BE YOURSELF. EVERYBODY ELSE IS ALREADY TAKEN.
♥ Oscar Wilde

CAR TALK

DRIVING IN ENGLAND

We have just driven four hours, a near-death experience, but we arrived in one piece with our relationship still intact—so I'm inspired to write about what we've learned about driving in England, in case it will help other travelers.

NO, IT ISN'T OURS, YET.

First off, if you are renting a car, get the narrowest one you can find; every inch counts on these threadlike cowpath backroads that often turn into one lane, even with two cars passing, to which I am sure the person who left their side-view mirror in the bramble hedge (above) would attest. You are almost always hemmed in by rock walls, thick hedge-rows, or buildings that front the road's edge. Our rented Volvo also has sensors that beep faster as we get close to a rock wall, or a car gets close to us; it's a big help.

I wouldn't even think about getting a car without GPS, what they call Sat Nav; it's a life line. So far, the comforting voice of the GPS announcer has never been wrong. Above is a photo of the screen in our car, showing our path through the next roundabout ... see what I mean? The GPS lady talks us right through it. If we miss our turn, we calmly go around again & catch our exit the next time.

132

Unless you specifically ask for an automatic shift you might be given a manual drive which means you would have to shift gears with your left hand. You will have enough to do just staying on your own side of the road, without that added confusion. (If you are British, renting a car in America, you will also want an automatic!)

I can't begin to tell you how important it is for the driver to remember that the larger portion of the car is now on his left. He should stay to the right side of his own lane & be careful not to run his passenger into a rock wall, hedge, or house, as she will very likely remind him however many times it takes. At the same time, the passenger should express her gratitude toward the driver for shouldering this harrowing responsibility.

Screaming is apparently unappreciated by the driver, even his own, but it is sometimes unavoidable. Feet jammed into floorboards doesn't stop the car. Joe reminds me, "Loose lips sink ships." (Translation: "Silence is golden.") I remind Joe that we are all in this together & to, please, get over.

More . . .

CAR TALK, cont.

Slow-moving sheep & chickens, horse-drawn wagons, farm vehicles, & antique cars are common when you round a narrow bend in the road.

Other little tips: ✱ Obey speed limits; just so you know, there are traffic cameras on most of the roads, so use turn signals & go very slowly through towns & villages. There are specific rules concerning the sharing of one-lane roads with oncoming vehicles; you will want to learn about them in a helpful pamphlet called "The Highway Code Book." ✩

Traveling is hard work. Everything is *ALWAYS* strange; staying home *IS* much easier; but this you do for inspiration, for challenge, for beauty, for growth, but most of all, for the memories. And I said to myself, it's a wonderful world. ♫

WE ARE HERE & IT IS HEAVEN!

Good Morning! It's
Tuesday,
MAY 29 10am,
and I'm at that table and
that's my view below! We just
got here after spending the
last few days with our
dear friends Rachel & Paul.
We all went into London — let me tell you about that
first (before I get into the WILDFLOWERS . . .).

135

This morning I heard on BBC: "Three thousand miles of Union Jack bunting has been produced for the Jubilee." And I just bought fifteen feet of it to take home to decorate for a Tea Party. ♥

LONDON VIA AYLESBURY

When it's 3 o'clock in New York, it's still 1938 in London. ♥ BETTE MIDLER

We drove from Tenterden up to Aylesbury — & after that, it's all a blur — of tea in Rachel's garden, checking out Paul's beehive, getting to know ALICE, their little wire-haired terrier; eating Ray's delicious Lemon Butter Cookies (she gave me the recipe!), doing the kitchen dance to French Café music while making dinner. We all, including Alice, took the train to London for an overnight.

The city was decked out for the Queen's Diamond Jubilee, flags flying up & down Oxford & Regent Streets, as far as the eye could see. Crowds of people, all so festive — the only thing missing was the Beatles on top of

one of the buildings singing, "Get Back, Jo-Jo!"

We ate at famous restaurants Dabbous & Nopi — but my favorite was the tea booth at Cabbages & Roses, the Marylebone Saturday Flea Market. The boys shopped while Ray & I took our tea & cake under the trees, talking

& throwing crumbs to sparrows hopping around under the table. A perfect day.

PAUL & RAY DID A GREAT JOB SHOWING US AROUND — THIS WAY TO REGENT'S PARK

When we got back to Aylesbury, we drove to Ray's parents' home, a 16th-century farmhouse where Ray grew up. It was wonderful to see Diana & Clive again (Ray's mom & dad). "Di" made us a picnic which we ate at a shady table in their front garden. We walked through fields of bluebells & wild orchids & I heard my first cuckoo bird! And I got to pet a lamb! They have horses, cows, & sheep. Ray's sister, Lucy, & her husband, David (& their four-year-old son William →), are farmers & cheese makers.

We played with William on the lawn & ate a delicious lunch of roasted chicken — for "pudding" (which is what English people call all desserts!), Di made bowls of juicy strawberries & stewed rhubarb, scoops of vanilla ice cream, drizzled with balsamic syrup. 🍓

Ray & I started our friendship as pen-pals; our letters brought us close, & now, twenty years later, we visit each other in our own countries & we know each other's families & friends. We think it's kind of a miracle. 💙

137

Tuesday, May 29, cont.

I was sad to leave – it was hard to say goodbye to everyone. Ray & I are kindred spirits who live too far away from each other. But she had to get back to her bakery, Paul had to get back to his law office & we had to go find Beatrix Potter (which we will be doing in about four days!!). ♥

There is no charm equal to tenderness of heart. ♥
Jane Austen

THE PEAK DISTRICT
Wirksworth in Derbyshire
"DARBY-SHUR"

When we hit the road again yesterday morning, we didn't have a plan; we'd left these days open for SERENDIPITY — I think we've found it! We drove north along roads marked "most scenic" on our map & happened upon a "vacancy" sign which turned out to be this wonderful stone cottage called "Weathericks." ★ Already I never want to leave here. We stopped for groceries in the nearby market town – saw a great antique store but it was closed. (Guess where we're going today!

I came downstairs this morning to find this peacock on the terrace, preening at his reflection in the French doors. Our cute landlady, Jean, who brought over a bouquet of roses for our kitchen table, said he lives here & his name is Darcy.

LATER

9pm. It was positively BALMY tonight. We ate outside; the sunset turned the stone cottage the color of marmalade. "Pudding, my darling?" Joe said, as he

slipped one of Rachel's cookies onto my plate. She tied them into little cellophane packages for us to take along. "Mais Oui!" says I. Here's her recipe:

Lemon Butter Cookies

c. butter, softened
²⁄3 c. granulated sugar
I tsp. vanilla extract
zest of one lemon

1½ c. unbleached flour
½ c. yellow cornmeal
¼ c. cornstarch
sugar crystals ("for extra crunch," but opt.)

Cream butter, sugar, vanilla, & zest, until smooth; add dry ingredients; mix until just incorporated. Use waxed paper to shape & roll dough into two 8-inch logs, (about the width of a cookie.) Wrap in "cling film" plastic wrap) & refrigerate for an hour or so. Preheat oven to 350°. Slice cookies about ¼" thick; put on ungreased cookie sheets; sprinkle on sugar crystals (or roll the logs in sugar before cutting). Bake 15 min., until slightly golden. Cool on waxed paper. Makes about 40 cookies. Can be rolled out & cut with cutters into teapot or heart shapes. Just YUMMY with a special cornmeal crunch!

139

May 30, Wednesday 4pm

"EXPECT A WET TEATIME." BBC

The Peak District is GORGEOUS! We took a long muddy walk, up high on the hill behind the barn, looking over the rooftops of Wirksworth below us, across to the houses clinging to the hillsides in the far view; farmlands & woods, like a patchwork quilt of greens, ribboned by winding roads. I came back, chilled to the bone, jeans wet up to my knees; took my book & had a long hot bubble bath. I don't remember the last time I used a line-dried towel! I dry linens on the line, but not towels; I thought they'd be too scratchy, but, not only do they feel wonderful, they smell like the wild flower fields outside.

Sitting with a cup of tea now, listening to the rainfall, watching BBC — Joe is making soup & I'm about to paint the new teapot I bought yesterday at at that GREAT antique store in town. (Yes! I bought a teapot! Now I just have to figure out how to fit it into my luggage!) It was only £8 ~ which is $15.00 in money-as-we-know it ~ how could I refuse? That store had WONDERFUL things. →

RAINDROPS ON ROSES & WHISKERS ON KITTENS

WE BRAKE for ANTIQUE STORES.

There were silver spoons tied with ribbon, lace tablecloths, delicate cups of Lovely china with borders of pink & blue twining flowers, Staffordshire dogs & bisque dolls, gold lustre

Painting my "new" teapot while watching TV — the 1953 Coronation of Queen Elizabeth

creamers & fluted cake plates, remembrance mugs with kings & queens, & jugs with proverbs from days gone by; enamel trays with men in top hats & women in bonnets, & shelves of old books decorated with flowers & birds.

HEAVEN

7am Saturday, JUNE 2

*D*arcy is pacing back & forth on the stone wall outside the kitchen window. Fog is coming up from the lake across the buttercup meadow putting soft focus on the hills & the farm just below us. I can hear the nature national anthem of springtime in England:

MY TOE HUTS BET-TEE

*T*he Jubilee festivities start today in London — "beastly weather" is predicted, but according to the BBC, that's not stopping anything — it's all anyone is talking about. And today is the day we're driving to the Lake District where we've rented a flat for a week.

Approach to Chatsworth

*T*he last couple of days we've wandered the beautiful Peaks, walked along the River Derwent, visited tea rooms & antique stores (where I found some great old nature books); we drank Peah-ci-da, slept like logs up here in this quiet country with the baaing of the sheep & the mooing of the cows lulling us to sleep. We toured a stately house called CHATSWORTH ✿, an amazing place — just the drive to the front door was thrilling — the house was FILLED with art & history — Thirteen-year-old Princess Victoria went to her first grown-up dinner party there.

...LOOK!...

WILD FLOWERS OF THE WAYSIDE AND WOODLAND

POCKET GUIDE

Wherever we went, flags were flying for the Jubilee ~ the next five days have been declared a bank holiday by Royal Proclamation & the whole country is having a party.

Yesterday we went to Stoke-on-Trent ★, which is where all the most beautiful dishes were made during the 19th century; the hometown for factories such as Spode, Wedgwood, Royal Doulton, Minton, & Johnson Brothers. We went there to tour the Emma Bridgewater Factory ★. I love their mugs & have lots of them so we thought it would be fun to go see how they're made. We set up the tour before we left the island. It was fascinating to watch the artisans & craftsmen using the same 200-year-old techniques as their predecessors. We got to design & paint our own mugs as souvenirs of our trip. We left them to be fired; they'll be waiting for us at home in Martha's Vineyard.

me & my cup

Darcy, our peacock, has gotten more & more friendly; Jean gave us some peacock food & we've been feeding him so he's always around. We think he has a crush on our other bird visitor, a pheasant. The other night we watched Darcy chase the pheasant all the way across the meadow, zig-zagging through the tall grass. Every few seconds, Darcy's head would pop up, he'd let out a screech, then disappear again, getting smaller & smaller until he chased the pheasant right over the hill ~ while we are ROTF LOL. OK, must go pack teapot ~ See you in the Lake District !

143

Queen Elizabeth's
DiAMOND JUBILEE
1952   2012
GOD SAVE THE QUEEN
E II R

ASHBOURNE

PETEY AT EMMA BRIDGEWATER

KEEP CALM AND REIGN ON

ARTIST AT EMMA BRIDGEWATER

Fresh Lincolnshire
Asparagus
£2.50 a bundle
2 for £4.50
3 for £6.00

PATRIOTIC FARMER'S MARKET

CROMFORD

EMMA FACTORY

GOODBYE DARCY, GOODBYE JEAN; GOODBYE STONE COTTAGE, SCRATCHY TOWELS, FIELDS OF WILDFLOWERS, GOODBYE GORGEOUS PEAK DISTRICT

OK ENGLISH PEOPLE, FOR YOUR OWN GOOD, GET OFF THE M1 (ALSO THE M6) HERE WE COME!

HELLO LAKE DISTRICT ☆

AMBLESIDE ☆

CUMBRIA • POP. 2,600

June 3, Sunday 9:00 am Good Morning! Very dark day — intermittent POURING rain.

We're finally here for one week in the Lakeland country that Beatrix Potter fell in love with as a child. So excited! I've heard it's usually crowded at Beatrix Potter's Hill Top Farm. Supposedly, you have to be there the minute they open & line up for tickets. Then you still might have to go away & come back — it's a little house with not a lot of room inside, so the tickets are timed. It'll probably be even worse today because of the bank holiday/Jubilee weekend, so we're not even going to try until Tues. or Wed. I know it's asking too much to have the place to myself — but it would be nice.

Leaving the Peak District yesterday, we stopped at Bird's Bakery in Matlock to get one of their famous Custard Tarts — I'm eating it now. YUM! We arrived here in rainy Ambleside last night; stopped at the rental office to pick up the key & directions to our flat. Only three times through the village, 'round the twisty wet roads 'til we figured out what "turn at the Bridge House" actually meant.

145

Packing, moving & unpacking are down to a science now. Our new flat is right in town, on the second floor of a gray slate building on a river (Stock Ghyll). We cross the bridge with the Union Jack (below) to get inside ⁓ the landmark "Bridge House" ✴ spans the river in front of our building.

Decor in this flat is breathtaking! modern with floor-to-ceiling mitered windows & a giant flat screen TV that takes up one end of the living room; there's nothing in here that isn't black leather or chrome; the table I'm writing on has chrome legs & a glass top. But it's a good location — if it stops raining, we can walk everywhere.

US
↓

Ambleside is located at the head of

WINDERMERE,

England's largest lake. This area, far north & quite close to Scotland, is, as you might guess, famous for its many lakes, which they call "meres" or "waters," & mountains which they call "fells" or "Pikes". From what we could see driving in, the Lake District is made up of many small villages with lakes & mountains in between ⁓ perfect for poking around.

Joe just turned on the TV. It's raining too hard to go anywhere which is kind of perfect because it gives us a good excuse to stay in & watch the PAGEANT on the THAMES in London ⁓ the flotilla of a thousand vessels, celebrating . . .

QUEEN ELIZABETH'S DIAMOND JUBILEE, the anniversary of her sixty years as Queen...

The Queen is famous for her love of Corgis, images of them have been a big part of the celebration.

Following the Queen's Royal Barge down the river was every imaginable kind of boat, from rowboats & sculls, to fishing boats & antique yachts, and all of them decorated: Union Jacks flapping, bunting fluttering, streamers streaming; cathedral bells ringing, horns blaring, whistles blowing, down the Thames they went, past the Houses of Parliament & Big Ben, past the London Eye (that huge ferris wheel), past the Tower of London under the Tower Bridge. Millions showed up to celebrate despite the rain which has gotten worse all day (stiff upper lip & all that rot) — all the bridges & both sides of the Thames were PACKED with flag-waving people. The cameras are showing girls in matching Union Jack raincoats, flag-painted faces, & every imaginable crown & costume you can think of — and because of the rain, hundreds of thousands of COLORFUL umbrellas.

All to honor their beloved Queen, who, in her late 80s, with Prince Philip, 92, standing during the entire pageant, in the driving wind & rain for something like 5 hours! There were two red-velvet thrones for them to sit on, but they never did. There was a cover over the barge, but it was very much open on all sides. I don't know how they did it.

1952

Super Troupers

147

Sunday June 3, cont.

After the parade was over, the rain had abated; we put on our raincoats & went out to walk around hilly, wet Ambleside. It's a lot like Telluride, Colorado — lots of mountain stores, hiking boots, rain ponchos & backpacks. We took our books & went next door to a restaurant to have a bite to eat. For "pudding," we actually had pudding — STICKY TOFFEE PUDDING — it's been on almost every menu in every place we've gone — like the national dessert. We've managed to hold out, until now. It's a sticky, date-studded sponge cake in a puddle of toffee sauce, served warm, with the optional (for some, but not for us) vanilla ice cream. Tears-in-your-eyes delicious!

Custard Tart for breakfast; Toffee Pudding for dinner — officially gigantic now.

OUR   NEIGHBORHOOD

148

EVER SO STICKY TOFFEE PUDDING

350°
Serves 12

BRILLIANT, and oh so veddy English!

Set cake in a puddle of Toffee Sauce; drizzle over a little more. Pass sauce in pitcher. Serve warm with ice cream or whipped cream.

Cake

1½ c. pitted dates, roughly chopped
¼ c. boiling water
1 tsp. baking soda
¼ c. butter, softened

1 c. sugar
2 lg. eggs
1 tsp. vanilla
1½ c. unsifted flour
1 tsp. baking powder
1 tsp. cinnamon
¼ tsp. ground cloves

Preheat oven to 350°. Butter & flour either a bundt pan or a 9"x13" baking pan, depending on whether you want slices or squares. Put dates in a bowl, pour boiling water over, stir in baking soda & set aside.

Cream butter w/sugar in a lg. bowl. Beat in eggs, one at a time, then vanilla. Measure flour into another bowl, add baking powder, cinnamon & cloves; whisk to combine. Alternately add flour, then date mixture (including liquid) to egg mixture (flour-date-flour-date). Mix well & pour batter into prepared pan. Bake 40-45 min. in bundt pan; 20-25 min. in baking pan, until tester comes out clean. Remove cake from bundt pan while still warm.

TOFFEE SAUCE

1 c. butter
1 c. heavy cream
2 c. packed brown sugar
1½ Tbsp. bourbon, opt.
3/4 c. chopped pecans, opt.

Melt butter in heavy pan, stir in cream & sugar. Stirring constantly, bring to boil. Reduce to simmer & stir for 6 min. Remove from heat, stir in bourbon & pecans. (Reheat leftovers over low heat, stirring constantly)

June 5 Tuesday, 8am

GOOD MORNING!

We have a lot of catching up to do! Lots has happened!

Yesterday, after a week of gloomy weather, we woke up to gorgeous blue skies. So, after breakfast & a long walk, we thought we'd go find Hill Top. Not to go in, it was after 1pm, we knew it was too late, but to get the lay of the land, see how far away it was, how the parking was, all that, so we'd know what to do when we went there for real.

So, off we went through the narrowest of the narrow country roads, mossy rock walls on both sides in a hem-you-in kind of undulating pattern that seemed imminently crashable. And because of the holiday & the sun, we shared the road with pink-cheeked hikers with poles, bikes, buses, & caravans (what we call RVs) plus double-parkers & drivers who felt the need to pass it all!

The road signs had such familiar names, Grasmere, Hawkshead, Keswick, Sawrey, Esthwaite Water, like words from a fairy book; locations I've associated with Beatrix Potter forever—but here we are & they really exist! It's exactly as if a cartoon character was becoming real before my eyes.

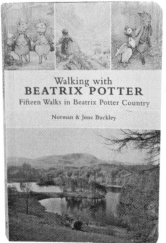

GOOD LOCAL WALKS BOOK.

It was hilly & lush, with shady banks of woodsy bracken & dense thickets. Ancient trees & huge purple rhododendrons framed lake views of sheep grazing near shore. We're driving slow & it *feels* like Beatrix Potter country.

Joe says, "See the rabbit?"

"What? A bunny? Where?"

I did not expect to be so giddy. I need chamomile tea.

We rounded a bend into a tiny hamlet & suddenly, without warning, we see a green sign that says, "Hill Top."

A parking attendant is right there at the entry & the very first parking spot is empty. He's waving us into it! Joe rolls down his window & asks him (because we <u>know</u> we're definitely NOT supposed to just walk into this place at 1 in the afternoon...),

"Is there ROOM in the house?"

"Aye," he says, his rosy cheeks puffing bigger with his smile, "just right!" English people are so cute.

Caught off guard, we look at each other, dumbstruck.

"Well?" Joe says, "Do you want to go in?"

I'm confused. We aren't going until Tuesday or Wednesday, this would be a change of plans. Suddenly, I shook the cobwebs out of my brain & said,

"What am I thinking?! YES! Let's go in! Of course we should go in!"

Common sense is instinct, enough of it is genius.
George Bernard Shaw

The two geniuses get out of the car & walk across the parking lot. I scan the roof tops of Near Sawrey. "This doesn't look like it," I say, thinking I would know what it looks like & wondering if we are in the wrong place. But there's the ticket office & only a couple of other people there. We're given tour books, & tickets for the 1:40 pm house entry. It's 1:20 now. OMG. This is it. I'm in shock. We are really, right now, going to see Hill Top Farm.

All my years of admiration for this woman came back to me. She was the first person I'd ever heard of that made a life out of watercolors, who had hand-written her own books. When I was younger, she was a big help in my search for my future self, in more ways than one. I found her through her art, but I didn't grow up reading her books. What really drew my interest was just HER, her story, the way she bravely overcame obstacles, honored her own dreams & became the person she chose to be, & made a difference

When there's an original sound in the world it makes a hundred echoes. ♥ John Shedd

Now we are the ones walking under the bright blue sky on a cool afternoon along the lane where Beatrix Potter once walked, past whitewashed cottages & tea rooms, decorated with Jubilee bunting & flower baskets, past a large meadow on our left, to a green-picket gate with a sign that says (gulp), ENTRANCE.

Beatrix Potter

HILL TOP FARM ✽

U p the stone steps we went, past the gift shop & down a long path. A fenced & hedged uttercup meadow is on our left, but I still can't see ne house. Joe nudges my shoulder & points; under a ree in the meadow are two bunnies grazing pictur-squely amidst a little flock of white lambs, & beyond hem, a far view of farmland & trees rolling out to the ills. BE STILL MY HEART.

he path has a cottage garden on both sides; clumps of old-fashioned flowers ran all over each other: lamb's ear, mint, & hubarb, roses, forget-me-nots, leeding hearts & wisteria. I valked very slowly, savoring. At the end of the slate ath was the house, very recognizable now..."As early perfect a little place as I ever lived in" is how eatrix described it.

weet as pie, exactly as I dreamed it, two-story 17th century, pebbly gray, with a slate roof & peaked chimneys & dark green trim around windows & door. The famous little front porch vas surrounded in pink climbing roses & adorned

the same way as the rest of England, with Union Jack bunting. This simple house was the place Beatrix bought the same year her fiancé got sick & died only one month after they were engaged. She spent years pouring herself into this house; it was her pet, her toy, her healing, & the doorway to the future she dreamed of.

A LITTLE HOUSE ~ A HOUSE of MY OWN ~ OUT of THE WIND & THE RAIN'S WAY. ♥ Padriac Colum

I was thrilled when I peeked around a garden wall & saw, on a windowsill, the same figurines that are lined up on the shelf above my kitchen sink at home.
I LOOKED AT MY WATCH: 1:38.

"I must try to make a fresh beginning," Beatrix wrote when she bought Hill Top.

Picture-taking wasn't allowed inside, but I keep paper in my purse for sketching emergencies & this was an emergency if ever I'd seen one . . .

154

T<small>hrough</small> the front door we went, into her kitchen first, where her straw hat hung by the cast-iron range. Her straw hat. And her farmer's clogs were on the floor in front of her spinning wheel. Just as she left them. Everything in the six small rooms had belonged to Beatrix & a lot of it was familiar because she used so much of it to paint into her books. She had prepared this house & planned for it; it was always going to go to the National Trust. She made Hill Top exactly how she wanted us to see it & left it as her forever gift. It's her living art. I stood in each room, taking notes & making these little drawings, but you are really going to have to come here yourself to be in her William Morris 'Daisy'-wall papered bedroom, in the company of her childhood dolls, & look through the same panes of leaded glass that she looked through, to see the view she saw — of the quiet countryside that had provided so much inspiration for her life. I stood there for a while & sketched her little 16th-century carved walnut bed, with the embroidered valance that Beatrix made herself.

"I have got a pretty dresser with some plates on it & some old-fashioned chairs."

BEATRIX POTTER

N<small>otes:</small>

B<small>eatrix</small> had special reverence for old, hand-crafted things. She bought most of the furniture for

her house at farm sales & auctions.
There were polished oak cupboards,
spoonback chairs & mahogany tables;
flowered teacups & plates & a
coronation teapot with a pink
crown lid. The charming green &
white wallpaper on the kitchen walls
covered the ceiling too. Light from
a large window illuminated the hand-painted face of the
grandfather clock on the stair landing.

INSPIRATION FOR HER "LITTLE BOOKS" IS EVERYWHERE AT HILL TOP.

In the room Beatrix called her "Treasure Room" was
her doll house ~ filled with miniature furniture
given to her by Norman Warne.

The decorations at Hill Top reflected Beatrix's love
for nature, statues, carvings, paintings, & wallcover-
ings, of birds, dogs, sheep, horses, cows, & flowers.

No one hurried us along &, in fact, the house did not
feel crowded at all. We stayed two hours and
had a wonderful conversation in the upstairs hall
with a twinkly blue-eyed National Trust guide named
Jenny Akestar, who shared her wealth of knowledge,
allowing us to pepper her with questions & volunteer-
ing all kinds of interesting details. She told us how
this renowned natural scientist & children's book author,
born & raised in London, had become a real farmer here
at Hill Top, & the pride she took in the prizes she won for
her rare breed of Herdwick sheep.
And, of course, all about the local
farms she purchased with the
money from her books, for
the purpose of restoring them
& saving them from development
& preserving the Lakeland
way of life.

The Victoria &
Albert Museum
in London
has her
original journal, 1881-1897,
written in code! Also the
original Peter Rabbit letter!

IF I HAD BEEN CAUGHT YOUNG ENOUGH, I COULD HAVE BECOME ANYTHING.
Helen Beatrix Potter

Beatrix Potter's encouragement & support was very important to the establishment of the National Trust. Beatrix was forty-seven when she married William Heelis, the tall, handsome, respected local solicitor who had helped her with her farm purchases. I thought it was nice & seemed important that the central offices for the National Trust are called Heelis.

Time Line

Beatrix Potter

Born in London July 28, 1866

'Little Book' Years
1902 - 1922

Engaged to Norman Warne
1905

Norman falls ill & dies
only one month later.

BEATRIX PURCHASES
HILL TOP FARM
in Near Sawrey
1905

She meets William
Heelis in 1908

They marry five years
later in 1913

Beatrix dies at age 77
December 22, 1943

William Heelis dies,
brokenhearted, eighteen
months later 1945.

Jenny also suggested a couple of other places of interest for us to visit: William Heelis's office in Hawkshead & a museum called Armitt that's very close to where we're staying in Ambleside.

After I'd walked through every room at least six times & microscopically examined every old photograph in the house; after I'd asked every question & had absorbed every fragment of inspiration possible from the experience; after I'd pressed every detail into my heart, we left, walking out the front door, blinking in the bright daylight.

Back along the garden path we went, taking pictures, hearing the birdsong, smelling the flowers. And then, to the gift shop. I bought a couple of little things for my Peter Rabbit room ✩, knowing full well this was not the end, I would be back. I'm not ready to say goodbye yet — look where I am & look how long it took me to get here! It would have been much harder to leave if I thought it was forever.

It's wonderful that Joe loves everything English. Maybe Beatrix Potter wouldn't be his personal thing in real life, but since she's a romantic, historical, antique-loving, English watercolor person, preservationist, from a darling town & a darling house (& since he does love me so very much), he seemed to enjoy this as much as I did.

Joe-B & me, we strolled, arm in arm, through the little village — stopping to take pictures of houses across Post Office Meadow & especially the house up the hill called Castle Cottage where Beatrix & William lived happily together for thirty years — you can see it in the photo —

CASTLE COTTAGE

I took this picture before I knew where she & William lived — but look! ← Doesn't that house just SHINE?

NEAR SAWREY

We walked by the overflowing window boxes of the Tower Bank Arms, a place where, many years ago, Jemima Puddleduck once waddled. Under the trees we went, to the Sawrey House Hotel. We sat outside, at a table on a stone porch & had a late lunch in the sunshine, watching a bunny nibbling leaves in the garden. Joe looked at his map, pointing beyond Esthwaite Water, showing me the location of Tilberwaite Fells & beyond, to the Langdale Pikes.

158

BUNNY IN

THE BUSHES

We marveled that some industrious person, a long time ago, had built a stone wall to fence in his sheep, now crooked & bent with old age, but still standing. It went on forever, straight up & UP & OVER the top of the mountains.

There are places I'll remember all my life...

ImaGinatioN: Painting Beatrix & her dog, Kep.

If you can dream it, you can make it so.

IN HONOR of BEATRIX POTTER, ELLEN TERRY, VANESSA BELL, VITA & HAROLD, RACHEL'S BACKYARD & EVERY VILLAGE IN ENGLAND, WHERE FLOWER BASKETS LINE THE STREETS... ☆

COTTAGE GARDENS

There is joy in the Spring,
when the birds begin to sing,
in an English Country garden

A GARDEN in TENTERDEN

Cottage gardens are everywhere in rural England; w
walk by them or through them every day. Bright old-
fashioned flowers, like tulips, hollyhock & sweet peas, free
mix with scented geraniums, strawberries, & chives, climb over
walls, spill into paths, peek out from door yards & border lamb
meadows. Fruits, veggies, herbs & flowers jumbled with sel
sowing plants like foxglove & sweet alyssum create a
little handmade paradise — gardens, both useful & beautiful,
the two best things in homemaking.

160

FAIRY MAGIC SPARKLES IN NATURE. ♥ LYNN HOLLAND

Everything in these gardens is made of natural
materials, wooden benches, bird baths, bee skeps,
twig teepees for beans & peas, wicker chairs,
straw hats, cut-flower trugs, bird houses & sundials.
Picket fences, rockwalls, trellises, arbors, pathways
& gates create charm & mystery.

Traditional flowers for an enchanting cottage garden
include sweet-smelling roses, lavender, bleeding hearts, cosmos,
clematis, nepeta, bellflowers, phlox, forget-me-nots, delphinium, sweet
peas, hollyhock, foxglove, scented geraniums — mix with chamomile,
mint, & basil, strawberries, peppers, arugula & tomatoes; a
lemon tree, an apple tree & something evergreen & round, to
create an anchor, boxwood or golden arborvitae.

This is the kind of garden that inspired my own small
picket-fence garden ☆ which, for such a little thing,
gives me so much ~ fragrance, beauty,
contentment, peace, & a bit of homemade
self-reliance; crisp fresh veggies for our
table, herbs to brighten my recipes, &
flowers for my vases. While I'm cooking,
I'll take my scissors, walk out to the
garden amongst the bees & the butterflies, cut chives, pick a sun-warmed
tomato, a couple of nasturtiums for
my counter & come back in to the smell
of roasting chicken, singing, "That's
the story of, that's the glory of love."

O THE GREEN THINGS
GROWING, THE GREEN
THINGS GROWING, THE
FAINT SWEET SMELL of
THE GREEN THINGS GROWING.
♥ DINAH MULOCK CRAIK

161

A PICTORIAL GUIDE
TO THE
LAKELAND FELLS
being an illustrated account
of a study and exploration
of the mountains in the
English Lake District
by
A.Wainwright

BOOK ONE

THE
EASTERN
FELLS

JOE FOUND THIS OLD HANDWRITTEN GUIDE BOOK

PUBLIC FOOTPATHS ABOUND

PRETTY AS A PICTURE

GRASMERE GINGERBREAD SINCE 1854

SAWREY
WINDERMERE

WRAY
WRAY CASTLE

One Happy Camper TAKING NOTES AT DOVE COTTAGE →

JUNE 7, THURSDAY 7 AM

It's been raining for two days — but as you can see, it hasn't stopped us. Rachel told us not to miss the famous gingerbread at Sarah Nelson's Bakery in the picturesque little town of Grasmere. It was delicious; flat, chewy, spicy. We deconstructed it as we drove along. I thought the secret ingredient might be candied ginger or grapefruit peel — Joe thought black pepper.

We drove around looking at the views, ducking into a few shops, reading in front of pub fires. We toured the home of William Wordsworth at Rydal Mount. We walked out to postcard-perfect Moss Eccles Tarn, the small lake where Beatrix & William would row on summer evenings (he fished & she sketched). She bought this lake & planted it with water lilies (& left it to the National Trust).

We had CORONATION CHICKEN at the Glass House (just down the street from our flat) ~ we had to try it when we heard it was served at Queen Elizabeth's 1953 Inauguration Lunch. It would actually be perfect for a proper English Tea Party, mounded in Boston lettuce leaves. Quantities depend on the number of guests ~ but, basically, start with 2-3 c. diced chicken; add minced red onion, minced celery, a quarter cup (or to taste) mango chutney, a half tsp. curry (also to taste), & nuts (either toasted pinenuts or chopped cashews).

On another bowl, add enough mayonnaise to bind the chicken; stir in zest of one or two limes. Thin the mayonnaise with lime juice to make a nice runny sauce. Add salt & freshly ground pepper; pour over chicken & mix well. Chill. This would be delicious served in an avocado half ~ I also think it would be good with grapes, chopped apple, or raisins.

163

MAP MAN

← EASEDALE TARN
KESWICK ↦

Found more things to squeeze into my suitcase!

BEAUTIFUL JAMS IN LOCAL SHOPS

THIS IS MOSTLY WHAT YOU SEE AS YOU DRIVE AROUND

June 7 · THURSDAY, cont.

Afterwards, we went across the street to the Armitt Library & Museum to learn about local history & to see the large collection of watercolors given to them by Beatrix Potter; the fossils, fungi, & mosses she painted around Esthwaite Water. In their gift shop Joe found a wonderful old book on the Lakeland Fells & I bought a beautiful handmade pottery mushroom, copied from Beatrix's watercolors; a TREASURE for my Peter Rabbit room. I also got a book called *Know Your Sheep*; apparently there are as many varieties of sheep as there are flowers. ALL of them ADORABLE. (Now all I want to do is paint sheep.)

Talking to the woman at the library, I learned that Beatrix never allowed electricity in her houses (only in the barns, for the animals); for her, it was all gaslight, firelight, & candlelight.

Rain or shine, today's the day we go back to Hill Top — we leave here early on Saturday, & Hill Top is closed on Fridays. Must GO.

Later 8pm — back at my table. It rained all day — but, in the local jargon, "No worries." Off we went to

DOVE COTTAGE

This wonderful house was the first home of William Wordsworth, where he did his "best work" from 1800 to 1808.

WORDSWORTH STREET
FORMERLY LEATHER. RAG & PUTTY STREET

Wordsworth, the Poet Laureate for Queen Victoria, gave the perfect advice for writers: "FILL YOUR PAPER WITH THE BREATHINGS of YOUR HEART" and "TO BEGIN, BEGIN." His cottage was tiny, probably built in the early 1600s, with flag-stone floors, little fireplaces in every room, small diamond-shaped leaded windows, funny nooks & crannies — a room that was wall-papered in newspapers dated 1800. There was a narrow passage to the upstairs; low ceilings & short doorways that Joe had to duck to get through; dark wood walls, a thickly whitewashed kitchen (so cute — I wanted to decorate it). There was a gorgeous view over slate rooftops from the back garden. We climbed the the wet uneven path to the highest point to look out over everything at the dark rain-stirred sky scented with smoke from log fires. There was a darling guide in the house with lots of almost gossipy information about the famous lives lived here. Charming — four thumbs up for this adorable place. I felt honored to see it.

AND THEN, TO TAKE CARE of UNFINISHED BUSINESS, IT'S BACK TO

Hill Top
because you're never too old for fairy tales

I wanted to find out the name of the rose over the door of the house, but even more, I'd walked away from the opportunity to purchase a special, numbered, limited edition of the first Peter Rabbit book, the one Beatrix had self-published. I didn't buy it the other day, even though the shop at Hill Top Farm, in the far north of England, across the wild Atlantic, at the end of a long garden path was the ONLY place on EARTH where this book was being sold. What was I thinking? (Sometimes I scare myself.)

166

It had started raining steadily & there was nowhere close to the entrance to park, so Joe dropped me off. I dashed across the lane, dodging puddles, & through the gate, into the almost-empty gift shop, where I purchased my little book. (I bought two—one to give away for my blog girlfriends ✳:) The clerk put them in a bag, then, trying to see out from inside my raincoat hood, juggling precious books, camera, purse, umbrella; aware of keeping everything dry, I splashed up the path toward the house. The rain seemed to have kept people away because, from what I could see, I was all alone in Beatrix Potter's garden.

Close to the house, I noticed a path I didn't see the first time. Veering off from the main walkway, it curved around to a green door in an old brick wall. Slowly I pushed it open, really hoping I wasn't going somewhere I didn't belong. I peeked in & saw that the path continued on the other side. I had to duck a little to go through because of the low, dripping lilacs pelting my umbrella with raindrops. I found myself in the walled kitchen garden I'd seen over the gate in front of the house, but now, I was on the inside, on a grass path

June 7 Thursday, cont.

that went past homemade hickory-pole trellises, with rows of beans & peas, neat mounds covered with all kinds of lettuce, a rhubarb patch & strawberries. The garden was enclosed by six-foot stone & brick walls brimming with lilacs. Invisible from the house (which is why I missed it before) was the white bee box Beatrix kept in an alcove ('bee bole') in the garden wall. I hooked the handle of my umbrella under my jaw & clamped down on it with my chin, trying to keep it over my head while I took a picture. (Harder to do than it sounds.)

Thank goodness I was never sent to school; it would have rubbed off some of the originality

BEATRIX POTTER

I left the garden & went back up to the house. The roses had a strong rich fragrance, almost David Austinish ✿. The young woman at the door said they were an old unnamed variety of rambling rose.

I felt like I should go. Joe was probably wondering where I was. As I walked back down the path of droopy flowering perennials bent by the weight of the raindrops, a thought came into my head, *you should take a flower!*

168

No! Really? Should I? Then I knew I had to, because, weighing the pros & cons quickly, it was clear I needed to press a real Beatrix Potter

flower into my book more than I cared if I landed in the Near Sawrey town jail. But I was careful; I didn't want to give Americans a bad name. I cased the joint first. (I have outlaw tendencies – Joe would NEVER do this?)

No one up the path, no one down the path. So, into the flower bed I went, reaching through dripping mock orange & climbing honeysuckle, imagining myself invisible despite yellow raincoat & red plaid umbrella. My thumbnail sliced through those rose stems like cake. I got two, one for each of the books I had just bought, plus a purple Iris for my diary.

An old mouse was running in and out over the stone door-step, carrying peas and family *in the wood. Pet* *the way to the gate,* *such a large pea in her* *she could not answer. She only shook her head at him. Peter began to cry again.*

I tucked the wet flowers, gently, ever so carefully, into my raincoat pocket, moving nonchalantly, before anyone could say, "Excuse me," (English people are so polite), "do you need help out of the bushes?" The only clue I left was a trail of muddy footprints, soon to be washed away by the continuing deluge.

I didn't feel like I needed to go back into the house; it was already permanently woven into the fabric of my heart. I know, some day, when my feet fail me & my legs don't want to go anymore, I will remember the view of the green hills through the wavy panes of glass in Beatrix Potter's bed-room, the smell of the rain, the soft bleating of the lambs &

that I'd been lucky enough to be all alone in Beatrix's cottage garden. Those little flowers (& this diary) will be the slender threads that attach me there forever.

gently clicked the latch shut on the green gate as I left for the last time. I turned & there was my honeyman who brought me here, sitting in the car across the road, in the rain, waiting patiently, reading his paper. I stopped for a moment to look once more across Post Office Meadow to Castle Cottage where Beatrix & William spent their lives together & took a deep breath of that rarified air. Joe leaned over & opened the car door.

"You OK?" he asked, peering into my face.

"I'm OK." I said, collapsing the umbrella & shaking

A REAL BEATRIX POTTER FLOWER

HILL TOP

- 170 -

it out before sliding into my seat.

"Oh, it was so wonderful, I don't know why I'm crying. Look what I got!"

I pulled the flowers out of my pocket & arranged them on the dashboard to dry. Joe clicked in a CD & Fred Astaire started singing, "Isn't this a lovely day (to be caught in the rain)..." ♪♪ Slowly, with the windshield wipers whooshing, our car wound through the tiny village, & away we went.

Last breath of sweets is the sweetest last. ♥ BEATRIX POTTER.

To HAWKSHEAD ✶

✱ HEELIS OFFICE · BEATRIX POTTER MUSEUM & GALLERY

THE NATIONAL TRUST

Hawkshead is only a couple of miles from Hill Top, along the narrow road that curves around Esthwaite Water. This, the smallest of the lakes, where Beatrix spent so much time roaming, is the place where William scattered her ashes one sad day, making her a permanent part of everything she loved.

Our car sheered through the rain water, tires slapping the pavement; bright green lines of moss edged the stony walls; cow parsley & buttercups tipped their heads as we blew by. We were going to tour William Heelis's law office. This time we were told it would be an hour before we could get in. Which left us time to explore.

171

Next time, I'd like to stay in Hawkshead; it's so old (10th century), you can feel the past, walking the quaint alleyways (strung crosswise with rows of of bunting) between the charming white buildings. Hanging baskets overflow with geraniums ; tiny gardens spring from every crevice.

I KNOW AN ENGLISH VILLAGE O SO SMALL WHERE EVERY COTTAGE HAS A WHITEWASHED WALL & EVERY GARDEN HAS A SWEET BRIAR HEDGE AND THERE'S A CAT ON EVERY LEDGE. ♥ E.V. Lucas

When we got inside the 17th-century law-office-turned gallery, we understood why we had to wait. It was so small, & tilted with age, like a grandmother's cottage in an old storybook. Low, thickly painted ceilings & walls, supported by

heavy oak timbers; twisty hallways, crooked staircase, tiny rooms with tiny windows, low doors & undulating floors: a perfect house for hedgehogs. Lots of Beatrix Potter's original letters, drawings, & paintings are displayed, showing how these offices morphed into water-color versions for Beatrix's books

Afterward, next to the fire in a nearby pub, we had a delicious hot stew of beef & potatoes & thick gravy, & watched the rain beat against the windows.

172

We shopped our way back to the car & stopped at a fun store called Stewardson's. They had the coziest cold-weather mountain clothes: thick, hand-knit sweaters made with the wool from local sheep; wooden walking sticks, heavy brown tweed pants, waxy slickers, sturdy boots & Wellies in every color. Plus, the cutest winter hats (except maybe that second one!) made by a company called OLNEY. All things for people who live in the true world of WEATHER.

JUNE 8, Friday 6:15 am

We leave here early tomorrow—today is our last day in Ambleside. And guess what? It's still raining. We should be grateful—there are 70 mph winds in some parts of England, but here, it's just gloomy & gray. Only one blue-sky day this whole week—that 1st day we went to Hill Top. We've not seen the sky since then — good thing a person doesn't have to SEE her lucky stars in order to count them.

I FOUND THE PERFECT TRAVEL PENCIL SHARPENER

I laid my Beatrix Potter flowers between paper towels & then between the pages of my HELLO Magazine — going to take Joe his tea & start packing. I have no idea what we're going to do today.

RAIN, RAIN, GO AWAY...

I began to forget when it hadn't been raining & became as one with all the characters in all the novels about rainy seasons who rush around banging their heads against the walls, drinking water glasses of straight whiskey & moaning, "The rain! The rain! MY God, the rain!" *Betty MacDonald*

Later JUNE 8, FRIDAY cont. 8 PM Still raining, but we did the most wonderful thing today. We were feeling penned up by the weather. We didn't want to just drive around, sit in a pub, or tour another house ⟶ we wanted to be outside in nature. So we went down to the ferry dock to look around & see if maybe we could get on a boat.

Normally, I think the dock would have been packed with vacationers, but because of the ghastly rain, it was almost deserted. There were lots of boats, all sizes including beautiful old wooden passenger ferries.

✫ WINDERMERE

The launches run all day, year-round, transporting people from Ambleside to other villages on the lake. We bought tickets to wherever the next ferry was going, not intending to get off, but just for the ride - to get out on the water. While we waited for our boat, we visited with the man behind the counter at the coffee shop & got take-away cups of coffee with shots of whiskey in them - perfectly egal. (And medicinal, for warmth & stamina, plus, The Rain! The Rain!)

Our ferry pulled up to the dock & we boarded under the most sinister of skies, with only two other passengers. There was an inside cabin with benches & lots of windows, but it was beautiful & wild outside, which is where we went, to stand under an overhang, next to the wheelhouse, talking to the captain, enjoying the sheltered view & cold rainy smell of the fresh breeze. A smooth ribbon of black water rolled out from the bow, while raindrops made overlapping, ever-widening circles in the water, as we crossed the lake to the other shore. The captain waved his hand across the panorama, indicating the acres & acres of wild-looking countryside in front of us, the rhododendren-copper beech-larch - & -birch-spotted woodland & meadows that had all been given to the National Trust by Beatrix Potter. He

KEEP CLOSE TO NATURE'S HEART & ONCE IN A WHILE WASH YOUR SPIRIT CLEAN. 💗 John Muir

made it sound like they love her here, that she's real to them. And why not? Her amazing gift to the country included fourteen working farms, plus another 4,000 acres of the Lake District to be kept undeveloped & forever open.

The launch followed the shoreline; we could see sheep grazing in the meadows that rolled down to the water's edge & branches of huge trees, bent low, trailing leaves on the surface. We chugged past a bird sanctuary w/geese, swans, ducks, waterhens & lapwings;

an egret flew in, white against the dark sky, his wings spread wide, skinny legs & feet dangling in the air. Birds, floating, standing flying, swimming, skidding in for a landing, all right up against the dark green shoreline, like a wild white zoo.

And beyond the timeless meadows & emerald pastures,
the rabbit holes & moss-covered oak & rowan trees,
& the "slippy sloppy" houses of frogs, the woodland-
scented wind rushed between the leaves & blew around the
gray veil that dipped below the fells, swirling up in a mist,
blurring the edges of the distant forest.

It must be the rain that made this place look so
ethereal & otherworldly. That white egret was
pretty wonderful, too. That's Wray Castle, where
Beatrix Potter came with her family for her first
visit to the Lake District in 1882. She was sixteen
years old — can you imagine her, exploring the water's
edge, then running up through the meadow to the castle
for tea? I can, too.

For a little over an hour we clattered along the shore, pulling up to small docks allowing passengers to jump on or off. It was perfect, a big drink of fresh air ⌒ communion with nature; we were rejuvenated. It was around 5 pm when we happily jogged through the rain across the street from the docks to the graceful old Waterhead Hotel, ✴ shaking ourselv off as we went through the door that said, "Bar & Grill." We sat at a table with a view of the lake & wondered: this building was here when Beatrix & William lived in Near Sawrey. Di they ever come here? We don't know. We ordered pots o' hot tea, leek & potato soup with the most delicious, crunch deep-fried leeks on top, & avocado-bacon salads. I got out my knitting & my diary; Joe pulled out his map. I excused myself to go wash my hands & guess what they had in the ladies room? You'll never guess.

Over the speakers, instead of music, they had a record ing of Judi Dench reading *PETER RABBIT,* in her precise & elegant accent with inflections in just the righ places: "*Flopsy, Mopsy, & Cottontail, who were good little bunnies, went down to the lane to gather blackberries but Peter (Pe-tah), who was very naughty (nawh-tee)...*" A children's book in a hotel bathroom. Is that just too much? I asked the bartender if it was alway there & he said, "Yes!" Jo went to the men's room & it was in there, too.

THE TALE OF SQUIRREL NUTKIN

THE TALE OF TOM KITTEN

CECILY PARSLEY'S NURSERY RHYMES

THE TALE OF MRS. TITTLEMOUSE

THE TAILOR OF GLOUCESTER

THE TALE OF PETER RABBIT

I love these darling English people! Who would do this? No one.

I've decided that England is the epicenter of CHARM. In people, architecture, traditions, gardens, books, & celebrations. They say things like "jolly good" & "dodgy." I think it would be fun if there could be a worldwide competition to see which country could be the most charming. Because if this charm "just happened" in England, unplanned, I wonder what we could do if we put our minds to it? Bunting EVERYWHERE!

England reminds me of a quote I read on a packet of Swiss Miss instant cocoa mix:

"LIKE A BASKET of DRINKABLE KITTENS, WRAPPED IN A BLANKET, NEXT TO A FIREPLACE."

And, that's it. Tomorrow, much too soon, we leave this enchanted, fairy-haunted place, where rabbits wear little blue coats. We thought, next time, we should try to find a cottage (with a fireplace!) on the lake; stay for three weeks, be very quiet, take many boat rides, maybe row under the moon & stars, walk hill & dale, & maybe never leave.

How did it get so late so soon? Dr. Seuss

179

Ideas for Music

TO GO WITH VIEWS of ENGLAND

American CDs work just fine in English cars.

↓

Vera Lynn~ must have!
Joshua Bell Violin
Jo Stafford~ "September in the Rain"
Bing Crosby "Isle of Innisfree"
French Cafe Music
Andrea Boccelli *Romanza*
"Ashokan Farewell" (for the Dales)
Edith Piaf "La Vie en Rose"
Frank Sinatra *with* Tommy Dorsey
Madame Butterfly Puccini

If you have a lucky mascot, bring him. You will need all the help you can get. ♡

The LAKE DISTRICT

WHERE WE WENT

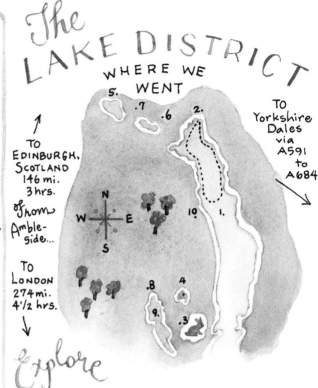

TO EDINBURGH, SCOTLAND 146 mi. 3 hrs.

of from Ambleside...

TO LONDON 274 mi. 4 1/2 hrs.

↓

TO Yorkshire Dales via A591 to A684

Explore

1. Windermere
---- our boat ride
2. Ambleside Armitt Museum
3. Near Sawrey Hill Top
4. Moss Eccles Tarn
5. Grasmere *for* GINGERBREAD
6. Rydal Mount
7. Dove Cottage
8. Hawkshead Heelis office
9. Ethswaite
10. Wray Castle

By Car

Ambleside to Hill Top: 7.3 mi. 18 min.
Hill Top to Hawkshead: 2 mi.
Ambleside to Grasmere: 4.6 mi.

Get a book on local footpaths. ♡ A gorgeous drive: When you're in Grasmere, follow the signs that say Elterwater or Skelwith Bridge.

Today we go east across the Yorkshire (Yōwk-sha) Dales. What is a dale? That's my question, too. So many different words for things in this area — like "fell" which means hill or mountain. At the Armitt, Joe bought a book about local place names & here's what it says: This area of the country was settled by Vikings in the 9th century — so here are some meanings for the Old Norse words we keep hearing: a dale is a valley; mere (like Windermere) means lake; a beck is a stream; a tarn is a small lake; a pike is a summit; there's a hill nearby called Elfhowe — elf is Old English for fairies or little people (so they obviously existed. I knew it), & howe means hill. Ling means heather-covered, so the place called Ling Fell is a heather-covered mountain.

Every child can remember laying his head in the grass, staring into the infinitesimal forest & seeing it grow populous with fairy armies. ROBT. LOUIS STEVENSON

One of my favorite books, *All Creatures Great & Small* by James Herriot, ✳ was set in the Yorkshire Dales. James Herriot's real name was Alfred Wight & he wrote about his life as a country vet in the 1930s & 40s. He referred to his books as his "little cat and dog stories," but they are much more than that. His descriptions of Yorkshire are so wonderful, he made me want to come see it for myself. He didn't leave behind a house for us to visit, but we thought we might stop in the town of Thirsk (known as "Darrowby" in his books), where his veterinary practice was.

They can't find my house now because I keep it quiet where I live. James Herriot

BOOKS YOU WILL LOVE

While I'm at it, I thought I'd give you a short reading list of books I've loved that will make your trip to England even grander. They are *Pride & Prejudice* by

181

Jane Austen (we're going to her house in a couple of weeks!); *Excellent Women* & *A Quartet in Autumn*, both by Barbara Pym; *Howard's End* & *A Room With a View*, both by E. M. Forster; *Enchanted April* & *Elizabeth and Her German Garden*, both by Elizabeth von Arnim ; *Bridget Jones Diary* by Helen Fielding; *Cold Comfort Farm* by Stella Gibbons; *Jane Eyre* by Charlotte Bronte; &, of course, *All Creatures Great and Small* by James Herriot. The list could go on but these will give you a jolly good start ~ & if you've already read them, then everything is tickety boo. (Another new word - not Old Norse - means fine & dandy.)

Later, June 9 cont. Saturday night, 11pm

A day in the car in an English county is like a day in some fairy museum where all the exhibits are alive & real. ♥ Rudyard Kipling

That is a very true statement! We traveled all day through the fairy museum, & now, I'm curled on a sofa in a hotel room in the walled city of York; it's late, Joe's watching TV. I want to write about today, while everything is still fresh. Sometimes, not knowing exactly where you're going or what you might find when you get there, you don't leave enough time. It was true for the Lake District & now it's the same for the Yorkshire Dales. After falling in love with the area around Ambleside & experiencing heart pangs while driving away, we were amazed that in just a few miles, we were into a completely different terrain, and falling in love all over again.

YORKSHIRE DALES

Let's see if I can describe it for you because, as pretty as these pictures are, they don't begin to do it justice ~ it's not that easy to capture magic.

182

roads lined in wildflowers

She Yorkshire Dales is a collection of deep river valleys formed by glaciers during the Ice Age. It *feels* primeval~if you walked out of there in 1756 & came back now, I don't think you'd see any difference in the landscape. Stunning views go for miles out to pinpoint-size stone houses clinging to hillsides, remote barns & crumbling out-buildings, sometimes with full-grown trees coming out of them. It's almost as manicured as a park, carpeted in buttercups & spotted with grazing farm animals. Rock walls divide pastures & disappear over the hills after crisscrossing the slopes, tracing patterns like a chain stitch in a huge patchwork quilt. The narrow road that cuts through The Dales is tightly bordered with shoulder-high wildflowers. May flowers & cow parsley hang over both sides of the dry-stone walls. Two-track rutted paths with grass growing down the centers cut between fields; hedgerows line river banks. Small villages & cottages with foxgloves peeking from dooryards come right up to the road's edge. We wait our turn to go over single-lane, arched stone bridges.

SAT., June 9 cont.

We stopped often, turning off the car engine to get out & lean on the walls next to meadows of waving wildflowers & bouncing lambs, to listen to the silence, to smell the breeze & to look at the view so big, it almost hurts your heart to see it.

England, with its history & air of magic, the soil & woods thick with meanings that survive in fragments, is an empire of imagination.

♥ T. S. ELIOT

AN "EMPIRE of IMAGINATION!"

The weather was like it was when we were on the ship. We could see storms coming from miles away, black clouds rolling across the valley drenching everything in a downpour, moving away quickly, leaving blue skies & high white clouds.

MIDDLEHAM
Castle

We took A684 across The Dales, turning right when we saw the sign to Middleham. We did this because the man who gave us the spiked coffee

at the dock on Windermere told us we should. He was so right. You know it's going to be special when you cross a river through a set of stone gates with crenellated (⊔⊔⊔) towers; we read that the first known settlement here was AD 69. Over the bridge & up the hill to the town center where there were ozy pubs, lots of bunting & flower gardens. We wandered around, stopping to admire the carved-wood sign for the

Black Swan Pub when we noticed a Union Jack flying high over the town above what looked like a giant chess piece. Broken castle ruins cut a jagged outline across the sky. Castle ruins! Right up the hill & around the corner. So, off we went, through a little neighborhood, where bright blue ceanothus ran over stone walls, pink roses drooped over doorways, & a white kitty watched us from a window.

← Castle Ruins!
Let's go! →

We came to a 12th-century castle we learned had been the childhood home of Richard III. Middleham Castle is set in a field of daisies; fairy foxgloves run all over the crumbling walls; it has an amazing view of the countryside, & they say it's haunted. So interesting! If you come here, you should leave time for a long walk up the track that runs next to the castle & have a little taste of the famous Wensleydale cheese & a pear ci-da at one of the pubs.

N.D.A.*

Looking down into the "Great Hall"

Farther down the road, we stopped to take pictures at a little farmhouse, got back in the car, were tootling along & suddenly found ourselves embroiled in a rare drama. Joe is leaning forward, peering into the rearview mirror, moaning,

"Oh no! Bloody hell!"

I laugh because these words are not normal from him.

"What's wrong?"

"I left the camera lens on the roof of the car. I just saw it fly off!"

"Are you sure?"

"I'm sure — I put it into that little padded bag; I'm going back."

We couldn't turn around right away, the road was too narrow & curvy; it was another couple of miles before we could find a good place to turn. Meanwhile, a dozen cars whizzed past us, heading right for the lens. We were sure it was being crushed to smithereens, the fall alone should have killed it. When we finally turn around, our GPS lady, who has her heart set on going straight, believes we are heading for disaster.

"Turn left! Turn left!" she exhorts.

Back we go, round the bends, scanning the road, & there it is, a speck of incongruously shaped black in the center of the two lanes. But again, we're on a curve between rock walls, there's no place to stop & get it. It's another mile before we find a spot to turn around again (making the day of the GPS lady). Now we are frantically formulating a plan for Joe to maneuver the car into the middle of the road, watching out for head-on collision, while honing in on the lens, continuing to move forward, with my door open, &

*NOT DOWNTON ABBEY

ne leaning out, trying to see under the door, scooping it p from the middle of the road . . . & that's exactly hat happened. We did it! And besides a little silver dent n one edge, it wasn't broken! It still works! So lucky! urn up the music & off we go.

ooking out over The Dales, I remembered the planetarium on the *Queen Mary 2* & how small I felt in the cheme of things ⌐ watching the shadow of the storm vercome the little farms, the long stone walls, reminded me hat what we do here actually does matter.

ou know what I just realized as I'm writing this? Everything I was looking at out there today was made by hand! All those farmhouses & barns, the rock walls, the castle, the entire town of

iddleham, almost everything was hand-made ⌐ before there were machines. y ancestor was born here in York-shire in 1590. He made his living s a weaver; if he hadn't left for America, part of me might be here, amongst the generations that stayed, doing what every-one who lives here has always done, farming the land, making cheese, shearing sheep, gathering eggs, growing vegetables & flowers, mending fences; I'd be saying, "crikey," eating puddings, & oing off to swim in the tarn.

here is a need that each of us should understand where they came from, what they are, and what will become of them. WULFSTAN AD 956 Archbishop of York

Cow Parsley from the Yorkshire Dales.

James Herriot
1916 – 1995

BUT THIS HILL REALLY WAS A BEAUTY, A NOTORIOUS ROAD EVEN
IN THIS COUNTRY. AS I NOSED GINGERLY ONTO IT, THE
WHOLE WORLD SEEMED TO DROP AWAY FROM ME.
JAMES HERRIOT

Driving in to Thirsk, it was easy to picture James
Herriot in his little car, the one with no brakes,
heading out to The Dales along narrow, muddy
paths in the dark & freezing night, to take care of a sick far
animal. Everything he wrote about The Dales was true — it
was as wild & "beguiling" as he said it would be. At the
end of Kirkgate Street, where he'd spent his life as a vet
(even after he became an author),
there was a large gothic church
where he & his wife were married
in 1941. We were too late for a tour
through the veterinary office, but
it was lovely hearing the
church bells on the
same echo-y street he'd
been on, this humble man
with a big heart.

188

LOVED THIS OLD JUG ON THE MANTLE IN BEATRIX POTTER'S BEDROOM

ESPECIALLY THE POEM THAT DECORATED IT.

♥

LET THE WEALTHY & GREAT
ROLL IN SPLENDOR & STATE
I ENVY THEM NOT, I DECLARE IT.
I EAT MY OWN LAMB, MY OWN
CHICKENS & HAM,
I SHEAR MY OWN SHEEP & I WEAR IT.
I HAVE LAWNS, I HAVE BOWERS,
I HAVE FRUIT, I HAVE FLOWERS,
THE LARK IS MY MORNING ALARMER
SO YOU JOLLY BOYS NOW,
HERE'S GOD BLESS THE PLOUGH,
LONG LIFE & SUCCESS
TO THE FARMER.

♥

From a 15th-century song

YORK

POPULATION 200,000

ON OUR WAY INTO YORK

Woke up to clanging church bells. Poked my head out the window to get the lay of the land. Our hotel is directly across the street from the awesome (& I mean that in the best sense of the word) York Minster, one of the largest cathedra in England. They started building this outrageous, amazing, wonderful (handmade) church in the 12ᵗʰ century & finished it three hundred years late

It's Sunday & the entire countryside is being called to church with the

TINTINNABULATION.

(Edgar Allan Poe made up the PERFECT word to describe the sound of cathedral bells.)

So we dressed & ran across the street into the cathedral for Church of England Sunday services. The angelic voices of choir boys & girls reverberated down the ninety-six-foot-long nave; the congregation sang, too ⌒ we sounded beautiful ⌒

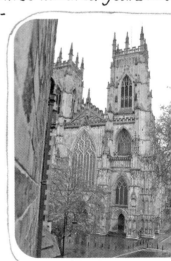

THE VIEW FROM OUR HOTEL WINDOW

the organ played & we thought about what it must have looked like in this church in 1500. Outside, there was a Roman column. York was settled in AD 71 by the Romans! Can you imagine? They came here all the way from Italy two thousand years ago. Seems like a long way to go for conquest. They must not have heard they could, as Beatrix Potter would say, "...warm their own hearts with the treasures of home."

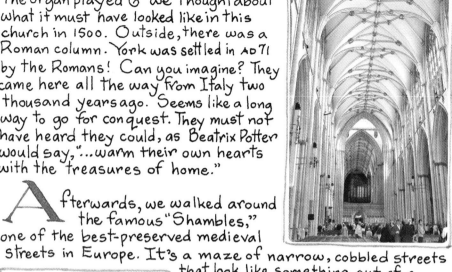

Afterwards, we walked around the famous "Shambles," one of the best-preserved medieval streets in Europe. It's a maze of narrow, cobbled streets that look like something out of a Dickens novel, with adorable half-timbered & brick houses hanging over the street. The spires of the Minster rise above it all, like a sparkly cake topper.

Why didn't anyone tell us about YORK? It's a wonderful little city ⌒ if I was twenty-three I might have to move here! There are musicians on every street~ across from the cathedral was a man on a piano, playing "Music of the Night"

from *Phantom of the Opera.* You hear the music & look up at the cathedral, & the towers aren't the only thing that's soaring.

THE
Cotswolds

N
W — E
S

Hidcote
•11

•10
7. • 8   9

5. • 6 •
4.

To York
from
Bibury
3½ hrs.
187 mi

Bibury to Bath
43 mi. 1¼ hrs.

BIBURY
1
3 • • • • 2

To LONDON from
Bibury 2 h
83 mi.

Tetbury
12

Bath
•13

Ramble through

1. Bibury
2. Kelmscott
   Wm. Morris
3. Barnsley House
   Rosemary Verey's
   Garden

PLACES WE WENT TO (AND LOVED)
LAST TIME WE WERE HERE
4. Lords of the Manor Hotel
   in UPPER SLAUGHTER. We
   had tea there. ♥
5. Bourton-on-the-Water
   has a miniature village!

6. Stow-on-the-
   Wold
7. Broadway
8. Snowshill
   House & Gard
9. Lavender fiel
   for GASPS!
10. Chipping
    Camden
11. Hidcote
    FABULOUS GAR
12. Tetbury
13. Bath

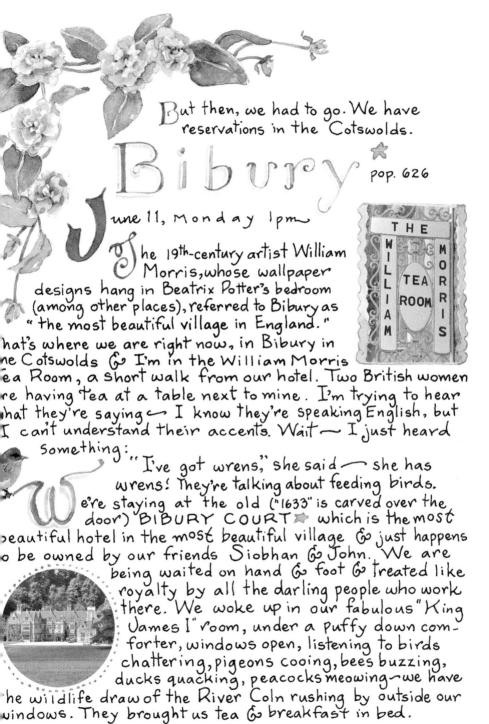

But then, we had to go. We have reservations in the Cotswolds.

Bibury ⭐ pop. 626

June 11, Monday 1pm

The 19th-century artist William Morris, whose wallpaper designs hang in Beatrix Potter's bedroom (among other places), referred to Bibury as "the most beautiful village in England."

That's where we are right now, in Bibury in the Cotswolds & I'm in the William Morris Tea Room, a short walk from our hotel. Two British women are having tea at a table next to mine. I'm trying to hear what they're saying — I know they're speaking English, but I can't understand their accents. Wait — I just heard something:

"I've got wrens," she said — she has wrens! They're talking about feeding birds.

We're staying at the old ("1633" is carved over the door) BIBURY COURT ✸ which is the most beautiful hotel in the most beautiful village & just happens to be owned by our friends Siobhan & John. We are being waited on hand & foot & treated like royalty by all the darling people who work there. We woke up in our fabulous "King James I" room, under a puffy down comforter, windows open, listening to birds chattering, pigeons cooing, bees buzzing, ducks quacking, peacocks meowing — we have the wildlife draw of the River Coln rushing by outside our windows. They brought us tea & breakfast in bed.

THE WILLIAM MORRIS TEA ROOM

193

We went out for a walk along the river & through the gar den. In less than two weeks we'll be boarding the *Queen Mary*. The thought makes me sad, our trip will be over — but then, a li thrill goes through me when I think of H♥ME & kitties.

TEA

Joe went off to an auction & I'm here in this tea room surrounded with flowery teacups & teapots.

One reason England is perfect for me is because (as someone once said) of the "heart-opening, wink-tippling" tea traditio which I love. It wouldn't be right to d a diary about England & not include tea! I learned to drink tea when I was around seventeen — I was intr duced to it by my best friend Janet's English mom Maisie. I would go over to Janet's house after school & Maisie would make us cups of tea & give us biscuits (her word for cookies I watched her fill the kettle with water, bring it to a boil & pour into a "proper" teapot. She pried the lid off a tin of loose tea & added a rounded spoonful for herself, one for each of us (m Janet, Janet's little sister Missy, & sometimes Janet's ten-year-old brother, George) & an extra spoonful for the corn flower-blue teapot she always used. She covered it with a tea cozy & let it steep for a few minutes, then she poured it through a little porcelain strainer into delicate china cups with saucers. I was so impressed! She taught us how good it tasted with honey & a "li'-o bi' o' milk." As we sat around the table sipping, Maisie would tell us about England & her sisters with the old-fashioned names — the adven-tures of MAISIE, FLOSSIE, WINNIE, GLADY, MARGIE, & JOYCE. I always thought they sounded so cute, like the bunnies in Mr. McGregor's garden.

194

Maisie served in the WAAF during WWII. Afterward she became a war bride, packed up her teapot & cups & came to America with her new husband. Her cozy kitchen, her flowered apron & our "children's tea parties" are a wonderful memory for me. Because of Maisie I not only found a lifelong love for the tradition of tea — I also got Janet & Missy.

TEAPOT'S ON, CUPS ARE WAITING
FAVORITE CHAIRS, ANTICIPATING
NO MATTER WHAT I HAVE TO DO
MY FRIEND, THERE'S ALWAYS TIME FOR YOU.

HOW TO MAKE THE PERFECT CUP OF TEA, MAISIE'S WAY

Maisie taught me that what makes a truly "perfect" cup of tea is the people you share it with. I know it's true — my girlfriends & I have solved all the world's problems over tea. Maisie liked black tea which is probably why I do too. I've tried it all, loose & in bags — these days I'm hooked on Earl Grey with lavender & rose petals. It's so good, it's like dessert. I even brought it with me!

Maisie showed me there's nothing mysterious about making a good cup of tea. Just bring fresh cold water to a boil, pour it over the tea & let it steep to the strength you like. Serve it with milk & honey,

195

Sweetness on a window sill in Minchinhampton ♥

June 11, Monday cont.
or half & half (highly recommend!), lemon, sugar, or plain, with nothing at all. Use a mesh spoon for loose tea, or an antique silver tea ball, a tea cosy to keep the pot warm — that's another thing I love about tea — the wonderful little bits that go with it — the teapots & mugs, saucers & cups, tiered plates & cake stands, silver spoons & linen napkins. These days, I invite my girlfriends to afternoon "twine." We start with tea & end up with wine. Maisie has no idea what she started!

TEA PARTIES ARE LIKE "PLAYING HOUSE" FOR GROWNUPS.

I like tea parties to *look* elegant, but *be* casual, because the first ingredient is comfortable happy guests. ♥
Tea party food runs the gamut of CREATIVITY; warm, homemade scones (pron. "skûns") with jam, "bu-uh," marmalade, Devonshire cream, & lemon curd, heart-shaped cucumber sandwiches, egg salad & watercress finger sandwiches, coronation chicken, & dainty treats like miniature chocolate eclairs, hot banana fritters, lemon squares, milk cake, chocolate-covered strawberries, & butter cookies. When I get home, I'm having a tea party in the garden with my new teapot & my Union Jack bunting! TWINE TIME under the roses!

England has lots of pretty tearooms. Years ago, we went to tea at Harrods in London. The table was layered in heavy, starched white linens, with napkins as big as pillowcases. The pianist played my favorite song, "La Vie en Rose." The teapots were decorated with sweet peas, the cups made that wonderful clunking china noise when you set them in their saucers. It was heaven. Those huge napkins made you wish you were wearing your white patent-leather Mary Janes, ruffled socks, & a full skirt with lots of crinolines.

THE DIAMOND JUBILEE - YEAR JUNE OF QUEEN VICTORIA

MY Li-o pride & joy.

Brew me a cup for a
winter's night.
For the wind howls loud
and the furies fight;
Spice it with love and stir it with care,
And I'll toast our bright eyes,
My sweetheart fair.
♥ *Minna Thomas Antrim*

Good to the last drop...

Must go now, meeting Joe to go take pictures
FOR OUR

Bibury Photo Gallery

We meandered through this rose-covered village along the river, past the trout farm; we walked with the gliding swans & followed the path through the churchyard rose garden. At the back was a blue wooden gate that led to our hotel . . .

Choosing the Photos is the hardest thing I do in this di

Because there are so many views in a

BEAUTIFUL village like Bibury

198

All wild swans, like this one, are under protection of the Queen. ♥

e River Coln runs through the village past our hotel (on the far side, below).

THE BIBURY COURT

This is our hotel! In her book *English Country Houses* (pub. 1941), Vita Sackville-West mentions that she loves Bibury Court. From the hotel, there are public foot-aths that go off in all directions. But the MOST wonderful ing, besides the blue fairy lights in the trees outside our

June 11, Mon. cont.

bedroom windows,
is the comfortable
DRAWING ROOM~
a big room full of
sofas, perfect for
knitting, reading
& diary-writing.
They brought us
a wonderful dinner
right there → in
front of the fire.
Afterwards, over

coffee, we had fun looking through this
1986 cookbook Joe found today. We were
looking at recipes, trying to decide which
one we should make first ~ "Soused Herrings,"
"Spotted Dick," or "Little Sodbury Lamb
Crumble." Luckily none of that was on the menu

THE COTSWOLD
COUNTRY COOKBOOK
MOLLIE HARRIS

tonight. Our dinner
was totally recognizable
roast chicken. YUM!

No long drive home,
just said goodnight to everyone,
then up the stairs we went. And look
what was on TV in our room — *Bridget
Jones Diary* — she's just about to kiss
Colin
Firth
in the
snow
♥!
One of
my

favorite movies ~ a perfect
ending to a perfect day.
See the twinkle lights out
the window? ... ♥

INSPIRING MOVIES

to see before you go to ENGLAND or any old time:

- Mrs. Miniver
- Miss Potter
- Howard's End
- andom Harvest
- Finding Neverland
- The Quiet Man
- ane Eyre (2007)
- Brief ncounter
- Young Victoria
- obson's Choice
- Sabrina (w/Audrey Hepburn)
- Love Actually
- The Secret Garden
- Mrs. Brown
- mma (w/ Gwyneth Paltrow)
- ver-After, A Cinderella Story
- ranford
- Scrooge (1951)
- hall We Dance (Astaire & Rogers)

TE: If going by ship, DO T SEE Poseidon Adventure h Titanic. And, btw, nerican DVDs do not work British DVD players. ♥

Walking in Bibury

Over the bridge, beyond

the hotel is a walk that takes you past a manor house, to lamb fields & poppy meadows.

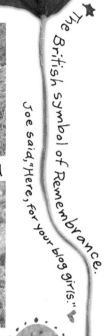

The British symbol of Remembrance.

Joe said, "Here, for your blog girls."

JUNE 12 • Tuesday 8 pm

*Have nothing in your homes you do not
know to be useful or believe to be beautiful.*
                    William   Morris

Today we drove about twenty minutes to
KELMSCOTT MANOR, an early 17th-century
house with lovely gardens where

WILLIAM MORRIS*
1834 - 1896

once lived. Before I landed in Southampton
six weeks ago, everything I knew about William Morris could
be summed up in one word: wallpaper. (And of course, his perfect
decorating advice, above.) But there's so much more, as we
learned today. He was an artist, author, & designer who
pioneered the Arts and Crafts movement in the last half of
the 19th century. We heard a lot about Arts and Crafts
when we visited Vanessa Bell's CHARLESTON — it's been
almost a continuing theme of this trip — the subject keeps
popping up. I need to read more about it, but basically we
learned that the movement was a reaction against the
Industrial Revolution, when people started leaving farms &
villages to work in factories.
Home goods, which were
previously handmade & reflected
the artistry of the maker,
were now being manufactured by
machine. William Morris
formed a partnership with
other artisans, rejecting mass-
produced home furnishings,

NEW WM. MORRIS "BROLLY."

I N THE MIDDLE AGES, EVERY CRAFTSMAN WAS AN ARTIST. ♥ *Wm. Morris*

encouraging conservation of the old ways, skills, & artistry. His company designed tapestries & embroideries, stained glass, tile, carpets, wall hangings & furniture. (The Industrial Revolution was to the 1800s what the computer is to us now. Some people liked it & some didn't, but for better or worse, it changed the world.)

We wandered through the gardens & toured the house — my favorite thing (inside) was the valance (called a pelmet) over Wm. Morris's bed — it was a lot like the one over Beatrix Potter's bed at Hill Top — a true work of art with poetry written by Wm. Morris & embroidered by his beloved daughter May with thousands of French knots (they didn't allow photos in there, sorry!). It was gorgeous — who wouldn't sleep well under beautiful words like these:

The wind's on the wold, and the night is a-cold,
The Thames runs chill
'Twixt the mead & hill,
But kind & dear
Is the old house here,
And my heart is warm
Midst the winter's harm.
Rest then & rest,
And think of the best
'Twixt summer &
spring, When all birds sing..." ✤ ✤ ✤

JOE IN THE WILD GARDEN

William Morris loved his home, he called it "heaven on earth."

June 12, Tues. cont.

I would say William Morris had the happy gene. Afterwards we had

tea in the garden with t birds & a yellow kitty who visited every table. I the gift shop, I bought a William Morris scarf— that's it ↑ up there, & a W.M.umbrella. Behind the house we crossed a tiny bridge & went for a long walk along the Thames Riv that flows past Kelmscott goes all the way to London We stopped at St. George's Church— under a weeping yew tree we found the graves of Wm. Morris & his family.

Driving toward Lachlad on our way back to Bibury, along a little count road with cow parsley & lambs decorating the

the roadside, we passed a sign that said,

"WEAK BRIDGE."

"Did you see that?" asked Joe.
    "What do you think it means?" I reply.
We looked at each other. We're in the middle of
   no where. Do we stop & go back?
Too late. By the time it registered, we'd just crossed it.

It was a great day but my favorite part was the
   kitty in William Morris's garden. ♥

I have to say, I'm so impressed with the generations
      of self-sufficient, hard-working, independent-
      minded, peace-loving, stone-house building,
brick-laying, flower-planting, rock-wall-piling, river-walk-
making, lamb-raising, farm-managing, foot-path-allowing,
tiny-arched-bridge-constructing, cathedral-climbing,
bell-ringing, hedge-planting, preservation-honoring,
history-loving, gravestone-carving, tradition-
   keeping, luv-lee English people, land-
   stewards who decorated this beautiful
   country so gorgeously. I'm glad I'm
   related to them! I hope they
   know how truly heavenly
   it is. If you are an English
   person reading this...

Thank You a thousand times for not tearing it all down to build something new, & for keeping the gardens alive & blooming long after the artists who made them are gone. I can't imagine how, when such things as indoor plumbing & electricity came into being, you managed to hold on to the character of these villages & towns while modernizing. But thank you. You didn't tear down all these luscious hedgerows to widen the roads for cars, & believe it or not, with all my complaining, I'm so glad. It's perfect just the way it is. ♥

O me! O me! How I love the earth
& the seasons & the weather
and all things that deal with it
& all that grows out of it.
♥ *William Morris*

June 14, Thursday 9pm
We're all tucked in at Siobhan & John's, but let me tell you about today at

ROSEMARY VEREY'S ★

garden

We packed up this morning & said goodbye to the darling staff at the Bibury Court who were so nice about our twelve (going on fourteen) bags & acted like they didn't mind at all bringing them back out to the car. We drove slowly through the village for one last look at the swans — then it was on to the next town where we'd made reservations for lunch at

arnsley House ⭑, a small
tel with one of the most
agical of the magical
nglish Gardens. Barnsley
use was the home of the
nowned garden designer
ROSEMARY VEREY
18 – 2001). The garden
't really open to the public;
order to see it you must
ke reservations at the
tel, either to stay there or for lunch or dinner.

So here we
are, for lunch, & a walk through
this garden filled with surprises. Flag-
stone walkways & lots of little gates
lead you through clipped hedges, past
knot gardens, perennial gardens, & a
tunnel of sweet-scented laburnum
underplanted in giant purple allium. Then,
out to the kitchen garden, redolent with
rain, thyme & rosemary. It's as
full of texture as a garden could be,
tiny leaves,
big leaves,

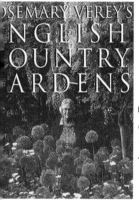

een, yellow, & silver foliage,
l things, short things, round &
nny things, tightly clipped &
wing in the wind, formal &
fettered; vegetables & flowers
jumbled together.

e came through an opening
in a hedge & discovered a
e with dozens of pale blue
ass bottles, hanging by their
cks, tied to branches with
ing ~ in each bottle was a
esh flower. It was a bottle
rden!

ROSEMARY VEREY'S FAMOUS
LABURNUM WALK

207

More Whimsy

The wind blew & they twirled. It made me miss my little picket-fence garden on Martha's Vineyard. We don't have the English climate but we have dirt ~ it's not bad dirt, we have sun, good sun! We have water! We can do something! Foxgloves & lilac love Martha's Vineyard!

And I'm going to plant lamb's ear.

Lunch was delicious & came from the garden ~ crunchy salads, fresh "al dente" asparagus, cold soup: leeks, potatoes, spring peas, blended with cream. Hot rolls, cold butter, cold white wine. Fingertips to lips, smacking noise, delicious!

TETBURY

SHIPTON MILL

We got here today around 3pm. I can't wait to tell you about our little cottage ~ but it will have to be tomorrow, because I can't keep my eyes open.

SEE THE LITTLE HOUSE AT THE BACK OF the PHOTO? THAT'S WHERE WE'RE

STAYING ~ IN THIS STORYBOOK

COTTAGE. WE CROSS THIS BRIDGE...

and go through Siobhan's garden to get to the Mill House where she & John live. Those are Siobhan's chickens. She hung the white bunting to keep the rooks away from their food. She put flowers & fresh eggs in the cottage for us. 🖤

THE MILL HOUSE

BY APPOINTMENT TO
H R H THE PRINCE OF WALES
FLOUR MILLERS
SHIPTON MILL LIMITED

Here's Siobhan ("Shivon") waiting for us in her fairy light ~ draped kitchen. (Don't you love her already?)

↗ (We love him too!)

That's John up there — he makes organic flour at his Shipton Mill by Royal Warrant to the Prince of Wales. There has been a mill at this location for a thousand years. Isn't that amazing?

June 17, Sunday 10:30 am

GOOD MORNING!

It's pouring rain. I'm alone in the cottage & happy because there's a little popping fire in the wood stove. Joe & John went off together this morning; Siobhan's gone yoga. I'm set up at the table where I've been doing a water-color of Beatrix Potter's clogs for this diary. I wonder why she never created a lamb character like Jemima Puddle-Duck or Mrs. Tiggy-Winkle. Seems odd since she did that with everything else ~ bunnies, geese, foxes, hedgehogs, even a pig ~ but no lambs ~ & she raised sheep! I would love a lamb figurine to add to my collection. I've looked everywhere for a really good lamb to take home, but so far my only choices have been key rings or stuffed lambs with crossed eyes & bony knees!

The cottage is without TV or Internet service which puts us on vacation from the real world even more than usual. The radio's playing old music while I paint ~ colored lights are looped across the room from a beam overhead. There's a deep bathtub, a well-stocked kitchen, lots of tea things, bouquets from Siobhan's garden, & a river running outside the window. A heavy velvet curtain pulled across the door blocks the draft. There are two bedrooms at the top of a winding staircase, rain beats against the windows & everything outside, past the hen yard & all the way up the hill as far as I can see is emerald green.

It's not down on any map; true places never are. ♥ Herman Melville

There's a pheasant under a tree out front staying dry.

June 17, cont.
Sunday

Siobhan, Tess, Joe, & John

We've been here before — the first time we walked into the kitchen of the Mill House John was standing on chair pouring boiling water in a huge conical canvas strainer filled with elderflowers & hanging from a rope & pul over the sink. He was brewin elderflower cordial. If you've ever smelled elderflowers, you kn how wonderful it was in that kitchen, filled with delicate wild flower fragrance.

How we met, in a nutshell: Years ago Siobhan spent a summ on Martha's Vineyard & we were introduced by mutual friends. She returned home to England, married John & raised two luv-lee children who are now in their twenties. They've all come to the island to visit us too.

ROYAL ASCOT✢

In 2004, John & Siobhan took us to Royal Ascot, the famous racecourse that dates back to 1711. It's too rainy to go this year, but I couldn't leave out this quinte sentially English event which was probably once-in-a-lifet for us. The Royal Family attends, festively circling the gras track with pomp & circumstance in horse-drawn carriages There's a dress code — gentlemen must wear top hats, striped pants & morning coats (with tails), & ladies should be attired in "day dresses" & hats. The men can rent their outfits, which was handy since we don't travel with a top hat; ladies, as usual, must come up with something on their own. Here we are, doing our best American version of a modern *My Fair Lady*

212

t was all we had to go on). Joe looking very elegant (& not s W.C. Fieldish as this photo might suggest~ (& me, I'm ist trying to see out from under that hat.

he event is quite a fashion show, the millinery was delightful; I saw a man wearing a 10nocle. Joe loves thorough bred orse racing but my favorite part f Ascot was the picnic in the "car ark" (parking lot) before the race. t's the English version of a tailgate irty ~ some people go all out, set tents (& have it catered ~ we had table (& chairs, a vase of pink ses from Siobhan's garden, deli-ious food, champagne (& elder-lower cordial. Best of all, Siobhan rought a wind-up record player hich played 78s ~ Edith Piaf singing "La Vie en Rose" French~old, crackly (& wonderful.

ince we arrived, Siobhan's been making the most amazing meals (& so much of it from her garden. Her igredients are all gluten-free (& full of healthy itamins~ she has a machine she loves called a Vitamix. She listens to Irish fiddle music while she slices (& dices under the twinkling lights (& sets out a brightly colored feast of fresh salsas, grated carrots, lemon-celery-root salad, sliced avocados, coleslaw, undressed "leaves" (that's what hey call lettuce), apple wedges (& organic handmade cheeses, ea shoots, quinoa salad, rice crackers (& gluten-free toast. And then we all just sort of graze. She made a POLENTA CAKE that I can't get enough of and she gave me the recipe!

Orange Lavender Polenta Cake

Moist Tender Delicious

*T*his is a huge cake – it can serve 24. You need a 12" cake pan (I used a large iron frying pan); you can also halve the recipe & bake it in a 9" cake pan which works just as well ~ you can also freeze it.

2¼ c. superfine sugar (you can make it by putting regular sugar in a food processor)
1 lb. butter, at room temp.
5¼ c. almond flour
2 tsp. vanilla
6 eggs
zest of 4 oranges (or lemons)
juice of one orange (or lemon; ¼ c. juice for 9" pan)

1½ c. fine yellow cornmeal or polenta flour
3 Tbsp. dried culinary lavender flowers (opt)
1½ tsp. baking powder
¼ tsp. salt

*P*reheat oven to 325°. Butter & flour a 12" cake pan. Beat the sugar & butter together until pale & light. Stir in almond flour & vanilla. Beat in eggs, one at a time. Fold in orange zest & juice, cornmeal, lavender flowers, baking powder & salt. Pour into pan, bake 45-50 min. until cake is set & brown. Cool 10 min., turn out on cake plate. It's delicious as is, A PERFECT TEA CAKE; also good with a fruit sauce & whipped cream. ♥

214

une 18, Mon. 7am
A rooster is crowing

GOOD MORNING

At this time of year it doesn't get dark until after 10pm, so last night around 7:30 Siobhan took us for a long walk, past Gloria, up the hill, through cow pastures, across wind-blown wildflower meadows, over field & stream, with fox & pheasant—Sunbeams streamed through breaks in the clouds.

Siobhan made "Gloria" to scare away rooks

Cows chased us!

She meandering foot-path brought us to a tiny stone bridge where Siobhan told us about the summer day she invited a few girlfriends to a tea party there. She asked them to bring their wellies & a waterproof chair. She put a table in the middle of the shallow river, brought blankets to make a picnic in the buzzing wildflowers on the river banks; she brought teacups, saucers, an old linen tablecloth, paper parasols, Sandwiches, cakes, a teapot, a vase for wildflowers & hot water in thermoses. Her guests wore strawhats & sun-dresses with their boots. She made tisanes from wild herbs growing nearby & set it all up on the table IN the river, right out there in the middle of nowhere. Walkers just happening by on the footpath were treated to this vision & offered cups of tea

This is Siobhan, adding her magic to the world. She does things like this, creates events, moments in time that just ∴POOF∴ disappear afterwards. She's like the elves I've written about on Martha's Vineyard, the ones that seem to run ahead setting up something beautiful for us to discover 'round the next bend. 🤍

Blessed are the happiness makers!
♥ Henry Ward Beecher

I think we're being followed...

June 19, Tues. 1:30 pm

Meandering through the hedgerows today, we've stopped at the pub at the Tunnel House Inn 🌸 There's a fire, comfy sofas, bunches of hops line shelves over bookcases, copper kettles hang from the beams, I brought along my new *British Country Living* magazine 🌸 ~ I think we may have to spend the day here! Joe's drinking a PIMM'S CUP (he makes these at home ~ recipe coming →) ~

I have tea and pear cider, chunky chips are on the way.

I haven't really mentioned how wonderful the pubs are. And I should. They're essential to the British way of life (and ours)!

Pubs

When you have lost your inns, drown your empty selves, for you have lost the last of England.

Hilaire Belloc

Drown your empty selves!" Ha ha ha! In 965, King Edgar decreed there should be one ale house per village, apparently starting a building-boom because even the smallest towns have at least one and the stone thresholds leading through the doors are worn in the middle from centuries of use.

The pub we're in right now is at the end of a long bumpy track where you would never expect to find anything — but, like the red phone booths, pubs are everywhere in this convivial nation. And historical — if you go to the house of your hero or your ancestor, then to the nearby pub, you know they were there too. You can sit, read, write postcards, all in a family atmosphere. There are easy chairs, books, pianos, they allow dogs (♥), you can listen to people talking (especially children whose little accents tinkle like the high keys on a piano). Everyone has been so nice — from the way we're treated, it seems as though English people like us as much as we like them!

217

The food has been great, they have "Pie Night" & Sunday Roasts, & Yorkshir[e] Pudding is almost always o[n] the menu.

Speaking of menus, they have different things, for instance, "my-toe-huts-Bet-tee" pigeon is sometimes on the menu — I just work around it because the chops, steaks, & vegetable dishes are delicious, with roasty-toasty potatoes & wonderful sauces.

PEACOCK PIE

A Miniature Anthology of GOOD LIVING

There are a couple of things to know about pubs: You order & pay for food & drink at the bar—there is no wait service for drinks & you're not expected to tip the bartender. If you're having food you can request a tab—they'll bring the food to your table & for that you can leave a 10% tip. Many pubs have a garden for al fresco dining; you seat yourself, & if you order a glass of wine you have a choice of "large" or "small." The bartenders are very nice & like to joke but a word to the wise according to *Britannica in Brief*:

DO NOT CALL ANYONE "MATE" UNLESS YOU HAVE SERVED ON A BOAT WITH HIM.

MY Joe's Fam[ous]

Tea · Coffee
£2·00

BEER Garden
Hot Food
TAKE AWAY Food

A BRITISH FAVORITE SINCE 1851, JOE'S FAVORITE SINCE 19[...]

PIMM'S CUP

Pimm's #1 is availab[le] in most liquor stores in the states. Fill a tall glass w/ice. Add one part gin to two parts Pimm's #1. Fill glass w/ half seltzer & half 7-up (in England it's called Lemon[ade). Garnish w/slices of fresh cucumber, orange & lemon—top w/a sprig of fresh mint & add straws. &

Cool & Refreshing

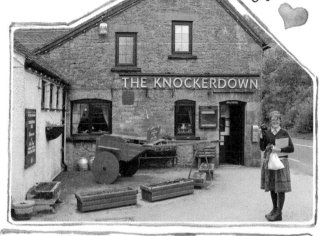

Children left unattended will be fed espresso and given a puppy!

SPECIAL MENU (INSIDE)

£8 6oz RUMP £8
STEAK
WITH CHIPS &
ONION RINGS

HOMEMADE LIVER & ONIONS WITH MASH/CHIPS WITH PEAS £6.95

ROAST DINNERS
BEEF/LAMB/TURKEY or PORK
SERVED EVERY DAY

STEAKS
GAMMON STEAKS (10oz)
AND MIXED GRILL

VARIOUS HOMEMADE
SOUPS SERVED WITH BREAD

HOMEMADE BAILEYS BREAD
& BUTTER PUDDING
OTHER DESSERTS AVAILABLE
ALL SWEETS £3.50

FULL ENGLISH BREAKFAST
BREAKFAST
PANINI'S (VARIOUS FILLINGS)
FRESHLY MADE OMELETTES
FILLING OF YOUR CHOICE

THE KNOCKERDOWN

Agency for
MORTIMERS
DYERS
PLYMOUTH

OLD FARTS
AND
WEBBED FEET
ONLY
CORNER

Kentish
Apple
Cake
£3.85

Fruit Scones
Cream &
Strawberry
Jam
£4.80

Ju n e 20, Wednesday 6:30 am

Thin veil of fog's puddled in the valley — black rooks rose in unison flapping raggedy-edged wings... Joe laid a fire in the wood stove last night so all I had to do when I got up was lay a match to it.

How do you like the lamb figurine I just made up? I'm calling her "Lambie-Pie Cuddle-Bunch." I think she makes the perfect friend for Mrs. Tiggy-Winkle. ♥ At least I have one lamb thing to bring home.

WINDERMERE

Sitting here wrapped in my shawl bent over the table, painting my lamb, waiting for the tea-water to boil: Beatrix Potter said she felt like a character in a Jane Austen book — if Beatrix Potter wrote novels, I would feel like a character in hers.

Hard to believe, only five days until our ship sails & so far we haven't moved a muscle in the direction of getting organized. If we're going, which apparently we are, we should think about how to get ourselves under way. We have to decide which places we can't leave this country without visiting — we have to go back to Sissinghurst for one thing — we need a schedule. Do I want to leave? No, it makes me cry to think about it. Am I excited about sailing past the Statue of Liberty, taking the ferry to the Island, seeing my picket-fence garden, burying my face in kitty fur? Oh YES!

220

DO NOT ATTACK ME WITH YOUR WATCH. ♥ JANE AUSTEN

Later 2pm — I

just heard a cuckoo!
Probably trying to
tell us what he thinks of us going!

We realized that if we want to get to Sissinghurst & Jane Austen's house, we have to leave here Friday — day after tomorrow! So we spent the morning doing laundry & organizing — now we're going for a long, old, muddy, rainy walk in the English countryside... then up to Siobhan's for tea — she's going to play the violin for us!

China tea ✿ the scent of

h y a c i n t h s

wood fires & bowls of violets

CONSTANCE SPRY

THURSDAY, June 21 • 11pm

Summer Solstice

And guess what? We went to the circus! John & Siobhan got tickets and the four of us drove to BROADWAY ✻, a darling Cotswold village about an hour from the Mill.
We had wonderful views along the way, lavender fields and yellow rapeseed ⟿ the houses are made of the most beautiful honey-colored local stone & the little villages all seem to be perched on cliffs with long views of the country below.

June 21, Thursday cont.

GIFFORD'S CIRCUS ✫

♥ IF YOU DO IT WITH HEART, THAT'S ART. ♥

is a family-owned, homemade country circus that's famous in the Cotswolds. We drove into town — there was a large, round white tent in a muddy field on Broadway High Street with colored streamers flying from the top. A rain-coat-and-wellie-clad crowd was gathering

around the handmade painted circus wagons, where popcorn, bags of hot nuts, cotton can-dy & souvenir circus mugs were being sold. We joine

GREAT BAND! about two hundred, young &

old, on long red-painted benches that went around th circus ring. There was an (almost) all-girl band, playing accordion, saxophone, trumpet, clarinet, piano, drums & fiddle. There was nothing scary or threatening — a Siobhan said, "It's terriers, not tigers." — no fire-eaters & the tightrope was about four feet off the ground — just fun & eccentric. Lots of stunts & running gags that included the audience; white doves & a hilarious dove-whisperer (I don't know what else to call her),

222

a darling goose named Brian; horses & ponies decorated in ribbons & bows cantering in a circle with costumed riders jumping on & off. There was a miniature TALKING PONY (but his handler explained he wouldn't be speaking tonight "because he's a little hoarse").
                  B a d a - B o o m.
There were leaping, back-flipping trick dogs, acrobats & jugglers ~ they had it all, not one bit corny, just charming, little & real. Many people have dreamed of running away with the circus — NELL GIFFORD really did & she brought us along. ♥

Gifford's Circus, by Nell & Toti Gifford, since 2000

"I held the jewel of my childhood up to my eye, & through it I saw ponies & a dressing-up box & a tent, & that was GIFFORD'S CIRCUS." N.G.

No worries ~ it all worked out!

THEY HAD EMMA CUPS!

··IT WAS A JOLLY GOOD TIME··

Watching this & thinking, "Don't go!"

223

June 21, Thursday cont.

STARS CLUSTERED AROUND THE CHIMNEY LIKE BEES IN A SWARM.
Marjorie Kinnan Rawlings

We got back to the Mill after dark, went inside for cake, then it was time to say goodnight — our last night — trying not to think about it. Joe & I walked back to the cottage the long way, over the stone bridge. The sky was clear & filled with stars. Arm in arm, footsteps crunching gravel, looking up into the sky, leaning over the bridge to listen to the river pour over the rocks. Then through the cottage door, draped with fairy lights, scented with roses & up the stairs to bed we go. Lucky Lucky People. 💙

. . . the lovely stars,
the forget-me-nots of the angels.
Henry Wadsworth Longfellow

SLEEP, THE DEPLORABLE CURTAILMENT OF
THE JOY of LIFE. 💙 *Virginia Woolf*

*J*une 22, Friday 7:30am — it's <u>not</u> raining, birds singing.

*W*e're up, car is packed, I've been writing postcards — here's the one I did for my sister Shelly — I did it in English English — hope she can read it.

June 22, 2012

POST CARD

FOR THE ADDRESS

£1.28

Commonwealth Games 1982

PRINTED IN ENGLAND

Hello Duck!
'Avin' a go-jus time.
Me brilliant bloke is gettin'
us through the dodgy "caw-pawks"
(but we're the ones doing the dodging!)
While I fancy the extra bits, biscuits,
ice lollies & chunky chips — all quite
luv-lee — Joe wants bangers 'n beans.
So far we haven't seen any crap-
jobs, but once again we're ex-
pecting sharp showers. I got a
new brolly & despite the beastly
weather, no one has gone barking
mad — although we had to say
blimey & even bloody blimey
because of the sodding rain. If
anyone gets cheeky, we sort it
out, have a quick kip & then we're
off to the weald to look for a pub. Wish you were here! xoxo

Michelle Stewart

*O*ur pheasant is back out front, Joe's putting together his magic bag (the bag he carries everywhere that always seems to have just the thing I need — from chocolate to extra glasses to stamps — he's ready for any thing). BBC Radio Four is reporting 4,000 people celebrated solstice at Stonehenge last night. "The leader of the Druids proclaimed it a great success."

*W*alking over to say goodbye to Siobhan & John in a little bit — hope I don't blubber all over every body. So hard to go —

June 22, Friday cont.

"I often think," she said, "that there is nothing so bad as parting with one's friends. One seems so forlorn without them." ♥ Jane Austen

We waved goodbye all the way up the driveway, they got smaller & smaller, then we rounded the bend & they were g o n e . . .

On our way to the ship . . . the lo n g way . . .

Going to squeeze as much wonderfulness into these last 2½ days as humanly possible. FIRST STOP: ★Lacock population 1000

This is the first of our "must see" stops before we sail away, this beautiful historical antique village of Lacock. Until 1944 this entire village was owned

226

by one person who, at the end of her life, bequeathed it to the National Trust. So it's been saved, loved, restored, cared for & is here for everyone to enjoy.

Because it's so authentic & well-preserved, Lacock has been the setting for lots of movies, such as *Harry Potter* & *Pride & Prejudice* (1995) ~ You might also recognize it as the charming village of *Cranford* in the BBC production by the same name. We walked all over taking photos & since a picture is worth a thousand words ~ here are a few thousand words ~ ♥

227

A fairyland of tender little leaves. 💜 Elizabeth von Arnim

June 22, Friday cont.
N E X T S T O P
Stourhead

💜 💜 89 Church Lawn ⭐ 💜 💜

The last time we were in England we rented this cottage from the Nat'l Trust & spent two unforgettable weeks exploring the surrounding 2,600-acre estate, with its hillsides of wild-flowers, masses of blooming rhododendrons & meadows of lambs. There's a 13th-century church where Joe learned to ring the bells, a pub, a manor house & so much more. One day we spread a blanket on the lawn right down there next to that bridge & had a long champagne-&-cucumber-sandwich picnic. People would all go home at night & it belonged to us alone, & at dawn too, it was all ours. 💜

That bridge is a grass bridge

WILD MARSH ORCHIDS

We came back today for a long walk...

228

STONEHENGE*

Driving east toward Sissinghurst, Joe surprised me. We've never been to Stonehenge; he never mentioned going there. I was oblivious as to where we were — just going along watching the sky turn pink when suddenly, there it was, looming up in front of us, unmistakeable — like all the photos I've ever seen of it! Sitting out there in a green field about a hundred yards off the road, where it's been for five thousand years. Mysterious, fascinating, but not a Druid in sight.

June 23, Saturday 7 am
Last night we stayed in an old hotel in Stockbridge called the Grosvenor Hotel ✹. White doves are cooing outside our window this morning. I checked the QM2 web cam ✹ on my computer — she's almost to Ireland — coming from New York to pick us up tomorrow.

June 23, Saturday
SISSINGHURST
THE JEWEL IN THE GARDEN of ENGLAND

VITA SAW HER TOWER
AS A GIANT SUNDIAL

Down the drive to Sissinghurst, between the narrow hedgerows still covered in white cow Parsley – it felt like coming home. This was my third time here but the first to see the White Garden in full bloom

IT WAS PERFECT

THE CHAMOMILE BENCH IN BLOOM

Tall delphinium & lark spur, tangled masses of Iceberg roses against red brick; phlox, balloon flowers & white bleeding hearts sparkled in the beautiful breezy day, flowing this way & that. We walked all through the garden again, through the pleached limes, out to the fragrant herb garden through gates & hedges leading from one amazing garden-room to another. We took lots of pictures & finally, reluctantly (& really, just so happy to have made it back), we said, Goodbye...

230

HAPPY TO SEE JOE OVER THE HEDGE

And off we went to Goudhurst & the STAR & EAGLE for lunch— where we are now, perched on top of a hill with pear cider & ploughman's lunch. We just got off the phone with Rachel & Paul. They went to Ascot, we asked how it was, Paul said, "Rain, beastly, bloody, sodding rain!" (He even swears cute.)

He went on, "I bet on a horse called 'Good Looking Man.' He lost by a nose." Ha Ha! Love this guy—asked him if he wore his ascot to Ascot. Tried to get them to drop everything & sail back with us. We almost had them, but then reality set in.

June 24   Sunday
Packed the car for the last time this morning —we're going HOME. At the hotel desk we got to talking to the Scottish clerk. When we told him we were heading home today on the QM2, he cocked his head & asked in a tiny voice, "Take me wi' yee?"

He was so funny we almost wished we could. He asked if we'd gone to Scotland — when we said no, he said, "Two months 'n' yee dint go a Sco'land? That's it, ah've gone off yee now." Loved him.

And then — off to the house of . . . 231

'Iceberg'

WHITE WISTERIA

Jane Austen

1775-1817

in Chawton

population 380

Run mad as often as you chuse, but do not faint.
Jane Austen

ST NICHOLAS' CHURCH
CHAWTON HOUSE

JANE AUSTEN'S
HOUSE

CAR PARK

VILLAGE HALL

Drifts of wild daisies front hedgerows & crowd the road to Jane Austen's house in the Hampshire countryside. And then, suddenly, there it was, in a small neat village of thatched cottages, brick walls & flower gardens. We parked & walked down the lane with nature's anthem, "my-toe-huts-Bet-tee" lilting softly from every tree, on our way to the rose-covered brick house with white-painted windows. I was so excited to get inside I had to calm myself so I didn't run anyone over.

Jane
Austen's
House
Museum

The 17th-century cottage was as homey & real as you would hope, as real & true as the characters in her books.

Worn-smooth wide-plank wooden floors, simple painted cupboards, practical little fireplaces in every room. And so many personal belongings — old letters & lots of handmade art, lace collars, portraits, watercolors, cross-stitch, a quilt Jane made — even a lock of her hair, her jewelry, teacups & silver teapot. The rooms were light & bright, cut flowers from the garden were on mantles &

232

June 24, Sunday 🚢 cont.
windowsills—it was charmingly
furnished—every room was
wallpapered in Laura Ashley
wallpaper (which was fitting as
Laura Ashley took inspiration
from old designs she saw at the
Victoria & Albert Museum, some
of which may have originally been
in this house).

It's a house to go slow in,
you can feel the reverence
& joy in everyone there,
leaning in as close as possible
to look at Jane's delicate turquoise

J a n e   w a s   h e r e

Which of all my
important nothings
shall I tell you first?
Jane Austen

& pearl bracelet, at her old letters & handwritten musi
at each tiny stitch in her embroideries, hoping to glean de'
of her life from the things she left behind.

Most of her personal letters were burned or censored by l
family after her death, so her short forty-one years on ear
left lots of questions. Her books, & the letters we do have, a

Girls in the hall

revealing, but the blank
spots in her biography w
filled in by her family wl
wanted the world to th
of her as an unremarka
retiring spinster. Since l
writings are anything b
unremarkable or retirin
there are differing opini
as to what her life wa
really like, which ha
spawned an empire of in
teresting conjecture in bo
& movies. I think of her
a normal, good-hearte
flirtatious, fun-loving, bra
girl who adored reading,
had a way with words &
became a wonderful sto
teller; a smart girl who li
life as it was handed
her. Two hundred year
after she died, her lig
shines brighter every day

Everything united in her, good understanding,
correct opinions, knowledge of the world,
& a warm heart. ~ Jane Austen

June 24 cont.

*T*he tiny table where Jane Austen wrote & revised her greatest stories was next to a sunny window in the break-fast room (near the teakettle). She wrote with a quill pen & ink. In the kitchen they provided quills, ink & paper & we were encouraged to try it. I couldn't wait to get my fingers around that feather. (Not as easy as it looks!)

I could only get about three letters written before I needed to dip the quill in ink again ~ I can't imagine how Jane wrote entire books in this manner, but I have no doubt, had I been living in the 19th-century, would have figured it out. You have to blot it too, otherwise it will smear. It's a slow process but I loved it — I bought ink & a feather pen in the gift shop. I'll save some space here & when I get home, I'll put a little of Jane Austen's writing philosophy there & I'll try not to smear.

Let other pens dwell on guilt and misery.

Jane Austen

Hello? Lois Just loved a house garden Wonderful

June 24, Sunday

Having ransacked the gift shop for everything "Jane," we lingered under the trees in the garden. Birds sang, bees dipped into the foxgloves; over our heads, dappled sun flickered through the leaves like a silent movie. Skimming a book I'd just bought, I was reminded again how everything is connected. In 1811, Jane Austen visited Chatsworth House (where we were a

few weeks ago) which she later described as Darcy's country house "PEMBERLY" in *Pride and Prejudice.* That's also where they filmed the movie; & why we saw a bust of Mr. Darcy at Chatsworth.

Then across the lane we went, to peek in the tearoom named for Jane's sister, "Cassandra" ~ my new favorite name. (If I had a lamb that's what I would name it.)

And finally, with no more excuses because our cup runneth over, & because the sundial was ticking, it was time to go. Really go.

We left Chawton for our final drive on the wrong side of the road through crooked lanes of old trees, hedges & wildflowers, as lovely as ever ~ we rolled down the windows for the cool breeze, turned up the music; Fred sang *Cheek to Cheek* ♫ "Heaven, I'm in heaven ♪," & we were.

OUR RIDE IS HERE

OCEAN TERMINAL

een Mary 2
HAMILTON

one 2

I'm sitting in there ↗ Joe went to return the car, I'm
waiting with our bags. The ship looms large through
the windows & I'm here wondering how I can say
good bye. To this slower way of life, to thousand-year-old
trees, to serendipity & discovery, to teashops, pathways,
history & stone cottages, to kitchen gardens in every
patch of dirt, cavorting lambs in wildflower meadows,
to darling people who say "dodgy" & "crap job" (who
drive cars like this ↘ & think it's normal). How
can you not love them? Well, you really have no
choice, you just do, don't you?

Here comes Joe, hat first,
up the escalator.
Even if I didn't
know him, I would
think he's adorable.
He brought us lattés.
Life is still good. ♥

Parked at our
237   hotel last night.

Think only of the past as its remembrance gives you pleasure. ♥ *Jane Austen*

QUEEN MARY 2

Seven days of suspended animation ahead of us. Sea bands firmly attached, life boats counted. They played "GOD SAVE the QUEEN" as the ship began to move (the same tune as "MY COUNTRY 'TIS of THEE"). After it was over there were three cheers, "HIP-HIP," said the loudspeakers, "HOORAY!" said the passengers, with tears in our eyes. Seagulls swoop & cry as the Isle of Wight goes drifting by, the Atlantic opens her arms for us & we slide right in.

Syllabub, tea, coffee, singing, dancing, a hot supper at eleven o'clock, everything that can be imagined agreeable. ♥ *Jane Austen*

And that's the way it is here too.

Long walks, salt air, misty horizon, fast-moving clouds, views to forever, moon like mercury glass; I dreamed I was walking up our driveway, looked back to see Jemima Puddle-Duck waddling behind me. Lavender tea with rose petals & breakfast in bed. *EMMA* on TV in our cabin (in French, which I don't speak, crying anyway

238

ecause certain things are
st universally understood, plus
almost have it memorized).

"MARRY ME, MY
    WONDERFUL
 DARLING FRIEND,"
Mr. Knightley says to Emma
in the orchard (as I sob
underneath my blanket).

Knitting, reading in the Chart Room, peah ci-da for lunch,
fternoon tea in the Queen's Room, dinner & dancing ~
he clocks go back one hour every night making the trip
ome a little bit slower. Which is good for "re-entry"— after
wo months away it would be too much of a shock to walk
it of 19th-century England, get on a jet, & fly directly
to 21st-century New York City. That might hurt, like a time
achine working in reverse. If England was a meditation
hich it actually was) this time on the ship would be the
unting-to-ten to bring us back to consciousness again.

Nobody minds having what is too good for them.
Jane Austen

STILL AT SEA

BUT NOT FOR MUCH LONGER.

Our last night, the after-dinner
    Grand Lobby tradition, passengers
    crowding the balcony & long
    winding staircases, singing old
ongs along with the piano — ♪
My Bonnie lies over the ocean...
and then... We'll meet again, don't ♪
   know where, don't know when...

A STOWAWAY
PERCHED ON A DECK CHAIR

239

The night will never stay,
  the night will still go by,
though with a millon stars
  you pin it to the sky,
  though you bind it
with the blowing wind,
  and buckle it
  with the moon,
  the night will slip away
like a sorrow or a tune.
♥ Eleanor Farjeon

In the pre-dawn came the first twinkling lights of AMERICA. We sailed under the Verrazano Bridge, waving from the balcony of our room to people in their cars. Then past the STATUE of LIBERTY, such an amazing sight, excited & happy, HOME HOME ~ we are H♥ME! One of the best things about going away is coming home.

240

H♡ME
Martha's Vineyard

We drove onto the ferry to the island just in time for sunset over Vineyard Sound. We stayed out on deck to see the JULY 1 lighthouse float by, then the white church spires, then OUR TREES (we can see them from the boat). It takes no time for the boat to dock, but today it felt like forever ～ so excited to be H♡ME.

UP THE BACK DRIVEWAY WE WENT,

Turned the key in the door, the smell of boxwood, welcome-home flowers from girlfriends in the kitchen. I walked into the dining room, Girl Kitty was on the table, she recognized me & began to cry, turning over, wiggling on her back for me to pet her. I picked her up & hugged her & I cried too. Jack is asleep next to me as I write this, his ball tucked under his paw. We slide right back into things here, as if we never went away.

But we did, you know. I've never considered myself to be an Anglophile. I looked it up & read that an Anglophile is "a person who's fond of British culture," which sounds mild but I always thought there might be a sort of irrational cultishness to it, so I wasn't an Anglophile, I just liked England.

Welcome home letter from my mom.

Now I realize an Anglophile is not made, she is born — in the gardens of rural England, in a tearoom on the edge of the Yorkshire Dales, & she can't be held responsible. It's like falling in love, she has to go with it. She sees an English Meadow in the middle of a stadium in London during the opening ceremony for the Olympics with real sheep & shepherds & geese & wildflowers & she realizes she's madly in love with the people that would DO that. She hangs up her bunting, turns on *Downton Abbey* & says, Sign me up.

To live is to be slowly born.
ANTOINE de Saint-Exupéry

I love the way Anna Quindlen said it: *A finished person is a boring person.*

So I'm homesick for England already. I can't stop thinking about everything we learned. I never really understood the Arts & Crafts movement before — now I have such an appreciation for it.

Not really for the "style" of William Morris's art per se, which has somehow attached itself to the phrase *Arts and Crafts* (which is what I always thought it was), but to his original idea, the honoring of handcrafted things & the people who made them, his quest to keep the HOME ARTS alive. ♥

And they are alive. Looking at that beautiful, mostly HANDMADE country — a sparkling jewel of castles, cottages, & gardens, I saw the whole thing as Arts & Crafts, built by generations of moms & dads, regular people going about their every-day lives, never seeing themselves as creative or special or heroes or anything like that, certainly not as artists. They were just doing what came naturally, making the world around them a better place.

Unsung Heroes of Self-Sufficiency

And I feel like I'm Arts & Crafts too — me & this homemade book. ♥ So are my friends — all my American quilt-making, cookie-baking, rug-hooking, chicken-raising, tree-planting, oil painting, scarf-knitting, scrapbook-making, care-giving, animal-loving, school-teaching, furniture-building, curtain-making, flower-growing, mural-painting, music-making, baby-rocking friends. ♥

My parents too —

243   KELMSCOTT KITCHEN

the mom & dad of eight, they taught me by example I could have anything I wanted as long as I made it myself. Do I want a roses-on-a-picket-fence kind of life? Build a fence & plant some roses. That's what they taught me ~ my dad who can build or fix anything; my mom who made something from nothing everyday ♥.

The ordinary arts WE PRACTICE EVERYDAY AT HOME ARE of MORE IMPORTANCE TO THE SOUL THAN THEIR SIMPLICITY MIGHT SUGGEST. ♥

Thomas Moore

There's surely a connection between the heart & hand & it shows in homemade things ~ it's what makes them unique.

Rachel takes her cookies & cakes to market every week like her grandfathers before her. She puts flowers from her garden between the pages of her handwritten letters before she sends them to me in America.

Her sister Lucy is farming & making cheese.

Paul tends his bees & builds a potting bench for his wife. ♥

244

Siobhan's chickens & vegetable garden provide fresh food for her family — she has tea parties in a river! ♥

John is milling organic flour in his eight-hundred-year-old mill: homemade bread made with his flour is served in his hotel & he makes elderflower cordial in his sink.

For most of us, making things with our hands is no longer a matter of survival, but we still do it. It's a way of giving. Straight from the heart to the hand & then out to the world. As simple as a jar of homemade jam or a child's drawing.

Nell & Toti Gifford made a small homemade circus & they entertain the countryside with it.

All the luv-lee artisans at the EMMA BRIDGEWATER FACTORY, working hard every day, making beautiful "pots" the way it's been done in that location for two hundred years.

Beatrix Potter painted her "little books," embroidered her bed coverings & kept the old farms going.

Because JANE AUSTEN was a woman, if she was to be published at all it would have to be anonymously ∵ but that did not stop her from writing thousands of pages with her scratchy quill pen. ᗺ

245

Modern-day stone masons maintain thousand-year-old cathedrals like York Minster, having mastered skills equal to their 13th-century predecessors.

The National Trust has hundreds of fine craftspeople, repairing, restoring & safe-guarding history for us, so we can go to these places & be PROUD & be INSPIRED. The National Trust motto:

"FOR EVER, FOR EVERYONE"

Statues at York Minster get T.L.C.

L o v e   L o v e   L o v e 💙

The whimsy & charm of CHARLESTON & the hand-painted lives of Vanessa Bell & Duncan Grant.

I was impressed when I learned about the great work PRINCE CHARLES does on behalf of the rural countryside. He's also President of the National Trust, a truly wonderful watercolor artist & has been promoting organic farming for over twenty-five years. (One of my treasures — even more so now that I've become a card-carrying Anglophile — is on the end papers of this book. It's a letter I received from Buckingham Palace in answer to one I'd written to Prince Charles's mother when I was eleven. Six degrees of separation :)

And then there's Maisie Campbell, teaching a young girl about another culture & doing it with something as simple & sweet as a tea party.

BIG & LITTLE THINGS · EVERYONE DOING THEIR PART, LIVING THE LIFE THAT GOD HAS GIVEN US. 💙

And now

Diana's seven-year-old grandaughter Alexis plans to write a book, & unlike Jane Austen she gets to use her own name. 💙

246

TEACHING & INSPIRING

Because the generations that came before left us a clear message: WHAT WE DO MATTERS.

It's the everyday little things that mean the most & make all the difference. What has lasted a thousand years? The beauty of man & nature is what has survived. The wildflowers & the countryside. The rock walls & the art. There are no ticker-tape parades for the people who built those cathedrals, planted those hedges, they never made the evening news, it's barely mentioned in the history books, but this is history at its most important, highest best. Perhaps just going about our business, thinking small, thinking HOME, thinking, "What do I have to GIVE?" is the true secret for a happy life.

IT WAS TRUE, SHE THOUGHT, THAT THE BIG THINGS AWE US, BUT THE LITTLE THINGS TOUCH US. ♥
Bess Streeter Aldrich

Joe built our little picket-fence garden—definitely one of my secrets to a happy life. ♥

247

We are the music makers,
and we are the dreamers
of dreams,
Wandering by lone
sea breakers,
And sitting by desolate
streams;
World-losers and
world-forsakers
On whom the pale moon
gleams:
Yet we are the movers
and shakers
Of the world for ever,
it seems. ♥ "Ode" 1874 ★
Arthur O'Shaughnessy

248

Making "music" in the Heart of the Home

What I learned & never want to forget for a

HOMEMADE HAPPY LIFE

Never say goodbye to serendipity & discovery, make room for them.

Walk a country road as often as possible

Hang towels outside to dry, make them deliciously scratchy

Take hot bubble baths with the windows open, a big glass of cold water & a good book

Listen to the Birds Sing

Visit homes & workspaces of HEROES for INSPIRATION & EDUCATION

Shop at LOCAL FARMS and farmstands for as much as possible: eggs, meat, milk, vegetables & fruit

Surprise someone you love, bake them a pie with a Homemade Crust

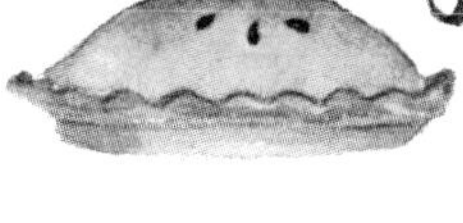

249

Grow everything to make ORGANIC vitamin-rich salads for your table.

Use kitchen scraps to make rich COMPOST to fertilize your GARDEN.

Shop ANTIQUE STORES for staples: cute *vases*, old *baskets*, embroidered *dish towels*, mixing *bowls*, wooden *spoons*, flowered *teapots*, old *recipe boxes* & *quilts*.

Twinkle lights look good everywhere, & year-round.

SLEEP UNDER THE STARS.

Plant an *Apple Tree*; lie under it in the spring when the blossoms begin to fall; make *Apple Crisp* in the AUTUMN.

Make JAMs & JELLIES from local organic fruit & berries for tea.

Take a KNITTING CLASS ~ they're FREE in yarn shops & then you can make someone a scarf. ♥

250

Pick tiny bouquets of flowers for your kitchen counter.

Meditate: Say sweet things to yourself & Count your blessings every day. ♥

Take a **DEEP BREATH** of fresh air before going to bed at night: take note of the stars & make a wish for the world.

Make a nice healthy dinner for your friends.

✴

Things to ask for on your

Birthday
★ ✦ ★

♥ Good hand lotion, bubble bath & soap
♥ a rose bush
♥ candles
♥ a pound of good loose tea
♥ Books (p. 181), Music (p. 180), Videos (p. 201)
♥ Emma Bridgewater cups
♥ A piggy bank to start saving for *Your Dream Trip*

HAVE A TEA PARTY IN A RIVER. ♥

A N D L A S T B U T N O T L E A S T

Take your magazine to lunch — you never know who you might meet. ♥

Hours fly,
flowers die
new days
new ways
Pass by
Love stays

Carved in stone
on a dovecote in the
Cotswolds ♥

(ONE) *Love of Life*

The ferry horn just blared, echoing over Vineyard Haven like the honk of a goose. Our kitchen doors & windows are open. The breeze from the harbor rustles through the wisteria & slides along cool wood floors making my bare feet tingle. It's summer on Martha's Vineyard ⟶ *Isle of Dreams*

Outside there's a cardinal on the picket fence; two butterflies are playing tag through the foxgloves.

I can hear Joe working in the garden, he's rebuilding the old rose arbor. Every so often there's the comforting cadence of his hammering — blending perfectly with the other neighborhood goings-on: kids playing down the street, lawnmowers, & the fragrance of hamburgers cooking on a grill. I put Siobhan's cake into the oven, poured two frosty pear ciders into our new EMMA mugs (yes, they arrived!), & took them outside, letting the screen door slam behind me, stepping around GIRL KITTY, who was happy as a clam, squirming in the warm sandy driveway, curling & wiggling like a giant pillbug.

THE BELLS ON THE CHURCH ACROSS THE STREET BEGAN TO RING...

Joe was tying roses to the trellis. I handed him his mug — we toasted, he took a long drink, looked at me with that twinkle I know so well & said in a little voice, "My-toe-huts-Bet-tee." ♥

253

AND THEY LIVED HAPPILY EVER AFTER

THE END

I N D E X

There's an Appendix waiting for you on my web site at www.susanbranch.com ⟶ links to everything, all you need to plan a trip of your own, plus fun videos & further information on the people & places mentioned in this book. When you get to my web site click on "I Love England", then "Appendix."

257

A FINE ROMANCE

"Do you know," Peter asked, "why swallows build in the eaves of houses? It's to listen to the stories."

♥ J.M. Barrie

notes

_____
_____
_____
_____
_____
_____
_____
_____
_____
_____
_____
_____
_____
_____
_____

The Sweet Life

Give me a moment, because I like to cry for joy. It's so delicious, to cry for joy. ♥ *Charles Dickens*

TWO TICKETS TO PARADISE

I WAS OVERCOME BY AN ATTACK OF
PATHOLOGICAL ENTHUSIASM.
♥ ROBERT LOWELL
265

FOOTLOOSE & FANCY FREE

SMILE

"I'm trying to arrange my life so that I don't even have to be present." ♥ Anonymous

THE BEST THINGS IN LIFE
AREN'T THINGS. ♡

271